The
FRIENDSHIP
BOOK

of Francis Gay

D. C. THOMSON & CO., LTD.
London   Glasgow   Manchester   Dundee

A Thought
For Each Day
in 1993

*Friendship is the greatest bond
in the world.*

Jeremy Taylor.

TIMELESS

JANUARY

I REMEMBER that year well. It had been a long, hot Summer, and everything in the fields and gardens was very dry. Even when Christmas arrived, the plants, trees, and hedgerows were still looking jaded after the long drought.

Then on New Year's Day we wakened to a world of snowy whiteness. It was all so unexpected and looked absolutely glorious. After breakfast, we put on our boots and trudged down the lane in the cold, bright sunshine. Everything seemed refreshed in the clear, clean whiteness — peaceful, expectant, happy and new, like the year ahead would surely be.

We passed the tithe barn standing beside a modern farmhouse. They seemed to be linked — the old and the new, working together in the present.

We walked home again, recalling our memories of the past with great hopes for the future. The past and the future were joined on that sparkling fresh new day.

Life was worth living — for the trees, the plants — and for us.

SATURDAY—JANUARY 2.

I WAS impressed with the address a young minister gave to the Sunday school children. He listed certain articles which bear a striking similarity to Christianity such as the lifeboat, the fire alarm, the telephone, the ambulance and sticking-plaster.

Why, he asked the children, did he find these like the Christian message?

Very simple, he explained. *They're all there when you want them.*

THE FRIENDSHIP BOOK

FINALLY, my brethren, be strong in the Lord, and in the power of his might.

Ephesians 6:10

NEW Year resolutions are not always taken too seriously these days, but I still believe in making them and trying to keep them.

Look at it this way. Either we're satisfied with ourselves the way we are, or we're not. If we are, perhaps we're too complacent.

And if we're not satisfied, well, New Year is the time when even the most cynical of us find ourselves looking back with a regret or two. If we don't like what we see, there is no better time to start trying again, for with renewed courage and faith we may do far better things in the months ahead.

THE Lady of the House and I used to visit a lovely little tea-shop at Wareham in Dorset. If one particular window seat was free, we always sat there, because over it was a notice, "Lawrence of Arabia sat here". He lived not far away from Wareham and often visited the tea-shop.

The other day I heard this story about him. He was riding with a party through the desert and his young servant got lost. The others wanted to carry on and leave him, but Lawrence immediately set off on his own into the wasteland to find him.

Now, when I think of Lawrence, I think, not just of a man of courage, but of one who was concerned for others.

WEDNESDAY—JANUARY 6.

HAVE you noticed how often cheerful people wear cheerful colours? I have only to see a red scarf, and I'm reminded of a certain memorable day.

It was bitterly cold and I had grumbled a bit when I had to go down to the nearest shop. There were several customers waiting in the queue, shivering and complaining about the weather, and I added my voice to the chorus. We had a "gloom" about the season, getting more and more chilled all the while. Then the door was pushed open briskly, and with a flurry of red woolly scarf, in came Jane with a wide smile, her eyes twinkling happily.

"I've just seen my first snowdrop! Just think, Spring is nearly here!" She unwound her bright scarf, and went on before anyone could speak. "And do you know, my garden robin has found a mate! He usually drives other robins away from my garden table — Old Bossy Boots I call him — but now he permits his chosen lady-love to share the crumbs I put out. Yes, Spring is nearly here, folks, and isn't it grand?"

Suddenly it was indeed! Snowdrops, birds pairing, nest-building, fledglings calling loudly for food . . . all came to my mind in a flash, and the gloom and cold of the day was instantly forgotten.

Oh, for more constructive, cheerful thinkers in this world!

THURSDAY—JANUARY 7.

I'M sure the poet Noel Scott had his tongue firmly in his cheek when he wrote these lines, but perhaps there is just a tiny grain of truth in them!

When it comes to spreading gossip,
Quickly, so it won't get stale,
Tell the female of the species
— She's much faster than the mail!

HEAVENLY HEIGHTS

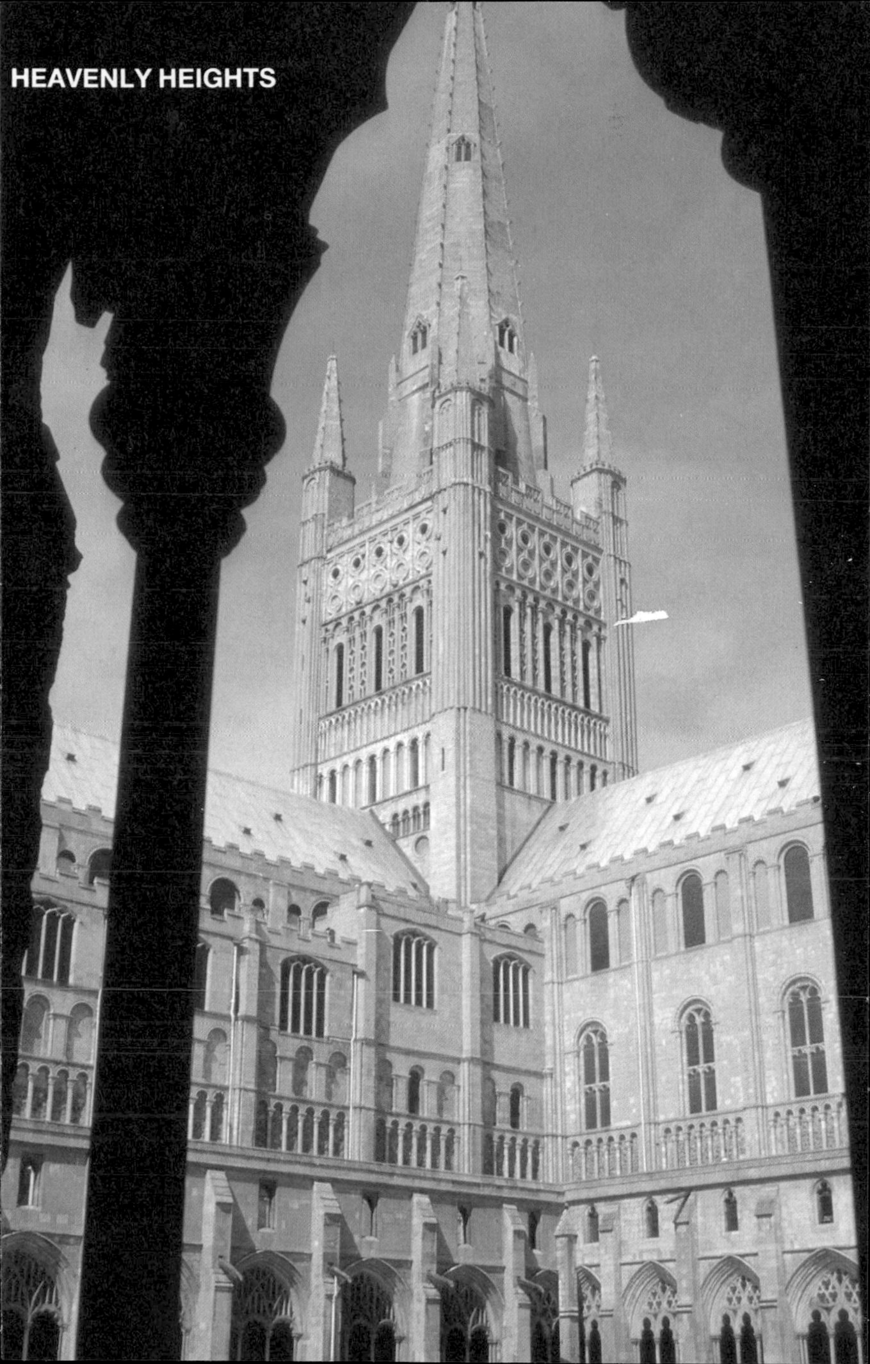

THE FRIENDSHIP BOOK

IT is always good to know when the needs of disabled people are being specially catered for, so I was pleased to learn that in Lichfield Cathedral, a "Touch and Hearing Centre" for the blind and partially-sighted has been installed just inside the great west door.

A large-scale model of the cathedral has been placed there complete with its three tall spires (the Ladies of the Vale), so that it can be felt in its correct proportions. The relief floor plan of the interior can also be traced by hand, revealing the layout of the building.

In addition, a tape acts as a guide round the cathedral and draws attention to the many places where you can stop and feel the stonework, statues, and carving on the choir stalls and Bishop's Chair. A guide book in Braille is also available for visitors, and often there is someone on duty to escort a blind person around the building and to make them feel particularly welcome.

PHYLLIS ELLISON wrote the following verse while in hospital, in appreciation of a newly-formed friendship, and I believe that many of us could relate it to our own experiences:

> *We shared our laughter,*
> *And our tears,*
> *We shared our joys,*
> *And sometimes fears.*
> *We shared our company,*
> *And in the end,*
> *We each of us,*
> *Had made a friend.*

THE FRIENDSHIP BOOK

AND thou shalt love the Lord thy God with all thy heart, and with all thy soul, and with all thy mind, and with all thy strength: this is the first commandment.

Mark 12:30

MONDAY—JANUARY 11.

ONE grey January day, The Lady of the House and I decided to tidy up the garden. The previous Autumn had been very wet and we were late getting down to the task. The remains of plants were drooping over the path, there was a smell of rotting leaves and, overall, an air of desolation. However, we worked on and at last cleared a path under our kitchen window.

There, hidden by some dead vegetation, we found a clump of fine green leaves. They were snowdrops, their dainty white heads just visible. It was a heartwarming sight, a fragile reminder that a re-birth was taking place in the earth.

This renewal surely happens in our lives if we allow it. When things seem hopeless, a small act of kindness or thought can start the cycle of positive living again.

TUESDAY—JANUARY 12.

AN early cup of tea in the morning, and then a warm, invigorating bath or shower. If, like many people, you enjoy these things at the start of a day, then be thankful that you belong to a society that has organised itself to supply water to our homes on tap, and to warm it for us.

Yes, we have so much to be thankful for. May we never take any of it for granted.

FINISHING TOUCH

THE FRIENDSHIP BOOK

<u>WEDNESDAY—JANUARY 13.</u>

I HAVE been reading an anonymous item about something most of us never seem to have enough of — TIME.

It was about the "Bank of Time" which every morning of our lives credits us with 86,400 seconds: "Every night, it rules off as lost whatever of this you have failed to invest to good purpose. It carries over no balance. It allows no overdraft. If you fail to use the day's deposit, the loss is yours. There is no going back. There is no drawing against tomorrow. It is up to each of us to invest this precious fund of hours, minutes and seconds in order to get from it the utmost in health, happiness and success."

On the same subject Arnold Bennett wrote: "We never shall have any more time. We have and we always have had all the time there is."

Father Jerome Le Doux wrote: "Every day is a new path on which to strike out, a new vehicle on which to travel, a new source of energy for us to operate."

How immensely valuable is each new day!

<u>THURSDAY—JANUARY 14.</u>

MY young neighbour Billy managed to catch me out again this week as we chatted over the garden fence.

"I'm a bit worried about going to Church this week, Mr Gay," he confessed.

"I'm sorry to hear that, Billy," I said. "What's the problem?"

"Well, it's getting a bit dangerous," replied Billy. "Last week there was a canon in the pulpit, the choir murdered the anthem and the organist drowned the choir!"

B

THE FRIENDSHIP BOOK

A FEW months ago, a friend of ours, Ellen, had a problem. She had just received an invitation to her granddaughter's wedding — but Joanne lives in Australia, and although an airline ticket had been included with the invitation, Ellen was extremely nervous about the journey.

"I'd love to go," she told us rather tearfully, "but I'm just not sure that I'm brave enough."

A few weeks later, Ellen came to visit us, and we were delighted to see her looking radiant.

"I did go to Joanne's wedding after all," she told us, "but I was so nervous on the plane that I kept looking at her photograph to reassure myself it was worthwhile. Then I started to chat to the lady sitting beside me, also visiting relatives in Australia, and we ended up talking the rest of the journey away. So not only did I have a wonderful time with my family, I've also made a new friend!"

Isn't it rewarding when we face up to something and find that fear is banished, and unexpected rewards result instead?

I LOVE to browse through old autograph albums. Amongst the humorous verses and carefully executed drawings a real gem is often to be found. Here is one I came across recently:

From the cowardice that dare not face new truth,
From the laziness that is contented with half-truth,
From the arrogance that thinks it knows all truth,
Good Lord deliver me.

A little verse — but a big message!

THE FRIENDSHIP BOOK

THEN he took the five loaves and the two fishes, and looking up to heaven, he blessed them, and brake, and gave to the disciples to set before the multitude.

Luke 9:16

THE Chinese have a thought-provoking story based on three or four thousand years of civilisation. Two coolies were arguing heatedly in the midst of a crowd. A stranger from another country expressed surprise that no punches were being thrown, but his Chinese friend replied, "The man who strikes first admits that his ideas have given out."

The story reminds us how much better it is to talk than to rush into hasty, and often disastrous, action.

WHEN I was a child, there was an aunt whom I visited regularly. Whatever time of day I called to see her, she always opened the door wearing her hat. She would welcome me indoors and take it off when we sat down for a chat.

Some years later, when I was less shy, I ventured to ask her why she always put on her hat before she answered the door. She smiled.

"If there's someone on the doorstep I don't wish to see, then I say that I am getting ready to go out. On the other hand, when there is someone I am pleased to see, then I say that I have just come in!"

I thought at the time — and still do — that it was a charming way to spare the feelings of unwelcome visitors!

THE FRIENDSHIP BOOK

TRUTH is stranger than fiction, they say, and here is a real life love story to prove it!

Peter French, a bachelor from Bristol, was a regular viewer of "Songs of Praise" on Sunday evening television. One Valentine's Day he watched the programme coming from a tithe barn near Tewkesbury, and his eye was caught by the lovely face of a young lady in the congregation singing "Lord of the Dance".

It was love at first sight and Peter made up his mind he would find her. Each Sunday he went to a different church in and around Tewkesbury and eagerly scanned the faces in the choir and congregation — but she wasn't there. Then, one day, he saw a notice saying that local choral societies were combining to sing "The Messiah" at Tewkesbury Abbey. Peter went along — and there was the girl. Her name was Sarah and he joined the same choral society, made friends with the girl who stood next to her, and soon they were introduced.

His perseverance and patience were rewarded and now Sarah and Peter are married — a very happy ending to this lovely story.

YOUR chin was made for keeping up,
Your hand for holding on,
Your upper lip for keeping firm
When all your luck seems gone.
Your head was made for holding high,
Your heels for digging in,
With this kind of anatomy
You're in the race to win.

Barbara Jemison.

ADVENTURE BOUND

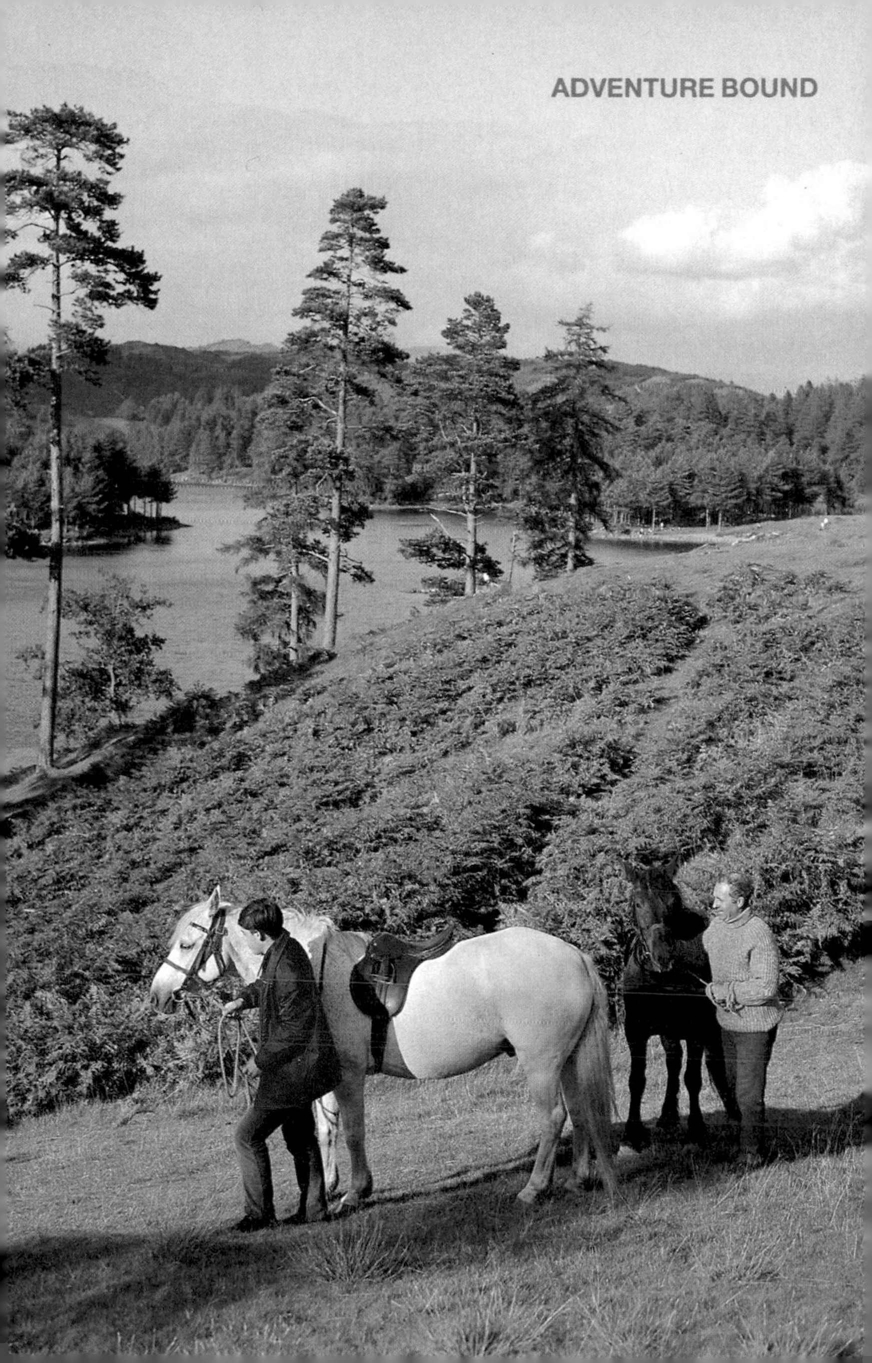

THE FRIENDSHIP BOOK

FRIDAY—JANUARY 22.

IN one of his books, Dr. William Barclay tells a story of how a small boy and his father who was a minister were exceedingly interested in railway engines. Where they lived a new church was being built, so their minds were occupied a great deal with this project.

One day, they were train-spotting when a magnificent new locomotive appeared. The minister — with figures on his mind — pointed out to the boy that it would have cost a lot of money to build: "As much as our new church will cost."

The youngster thought for a moment, then said, "I would rather have the engine, for I think it's worth the money far more than the church."

"How do you make that out?" his father asked.

"Well," came the reply, "the engine *works.*"

As Dr. Barclay points out, we have to make sure that both in our lives, and in our church, "the engine works".

SATURDAY—JANUARY 23.

WHEN the Lady of the House and I visited our old friend Mary, she proudly showed us her "new" ring. It wasn't really new, of course, for she has had it for very many years. It had become tight as her fingers had swollen with arthritis, and it had to be cut off and remodelled so that she could wear it comfortably again. Now it was buffed and shiny — yet still the same old ring.

As the years roll on we may find we have greying hair, less energy and perhaps need spectacles. But on the inside we are still ourselves, with all the qualities we are loved and valued for. Don't you find that reassuring? I know I do!

THE FRIENDSHIP BOOK

BLESSED be the Lord, that hath given rest unto his people Israel, according to all that he promised: there hath not failed one word of all his good promise, which he promised by the hand of Moses his servant.

Kings I 8:56

MONDAY—JANUARY 25.

SOME people are fascinated by long words; indeed, some like to show off by using the longest and most obscure words they can find.

A striking feature of Robert Burns's poem, "My love is like a red, red rose" has recently been pointed out to me. It is one of the world's loveliest poems, yet it contains only seven words of more than one syllable.

Long words may be impressive, but simple words can say much, much more.

TUESDAY—JANUARY 26.

*L*OOKING *back on childhood days*
Fond memories remain always,
Of Summer's playful hours of gold
And Winter's icing, crisp and cold,
Of dusty lanes and shady dells
And quiet Sundays' distant bells,
Of firelight flickering from the hearth,
A kitchen range, an old tin bath,
Of Dime, my dog, my faithful friend
On whom I knew I could depend,
Of Father's humour, Mother's love
And simple faith in God above;
Happy days, and though they're gone,
In my mind's eye they still live on.

Elizabeth Bloomfield.

THE FRIENDSHIP BOOK

IT was good to see the large placard on the door of the village church we were visiting:

"This is the gate of heaven. Enter you all by this door."

But we couldn't help smiling when we read the smaller notice placed underneath it:

"This door is kept locked because of draughts. Please use the back entrance."

I HAVE recently been reading the inspiring story of Dr Sheila Cassidy. After completing her medical training, she set off in a cargo boat to work in hospitals in the slums of Santiago in Chile. In 1973 she was caught in the military coup there and hit the headlines when she was arrested by the secret police, thrown into prison and tortured before her release was secured by the British Embassy.

It is often said that every experience of life has a purpose and shapes our future. Sheila Cassidy became the medical director of a hospice, where it is said she had an uncanny ability to find a new way of helping a patient when others had run out of ideas. The true meaning of hospice is "a resting place", and safety, love and comfort are what patients and families alike experience under her care.

Was this all quite by chance? I think not, and I quote Sheila Cassidy's own words:

"In my spare time I do a bit of religious broadcasting and preach in churches and cathedrals, often on suffering and prayer. My belief in God gives me enormous strength and joy and underpins everything I do. Daily prayer is as important as food to me."

FRIDAY—JANUARY 29.

IN the fairytales that were read to me in childhood, I remember that whenever a royal prince or princess was born, the fairy godmother appeared at the christening, waved her magic wand and bestowed gifts such as health, wealth, beauty and happiness on the new baby before disappearing in a puff of smoke.

Nowadays, godparents usually offer more tangible signs of their good intentions towards their godchild in the form of a useful gift. Some time ago, I watched as a craftsman displayed some of the items he had made with christening presents in mind. On a carefully designed child's dinner plate he had inscribed:

"Receive the child in joy;
Educate him in love;
Send him forth in freedom."

What better gift for any child!

SATURDAY—JANUARY 30.

THERE'S an old story about a man with a philosophical turn of mind who started to cross a road. Right in the middle he stopped because he couldn't decide whether it would be better to put his right foot forward next, or his left. As he pondered on the problem, he was knocked down by a passing bus.

The moral here is that it is surely sometimes less harmful to make the wrong decision than none at all.

SUNDAY—JANUARY 31.

AND in every work that he began in the service of the house of God, and in the law, and in the commandments, to seek his God, he did it with all his heart, and prospered.

Chronicles II 31:21

FEBRUARY

IN February 1990 someone rather special was given an Honorary Degree at Keele University on his 75th birthday. The man being honoured was Sir Stanley Matthews, the famous footballer.

He was interviewed afterwards and was asked, "Sir Stanley, you must have felt very proud and elated every time you scored a goal?"

"No, I never did," came the quiet reply. "What I liked best was to run down the right wing with the ball. I got a great feeling of elation when I passed it to somebody else, giving him the chance to kick it into goal."

He had been trained to work as part of a team and never sought personal glory.

What he felt is true of life, too. By ourselves we can achieve little, but if we work closely with others, sharing our skills, isn't it amazing what can be done?

DO you ever say, "Touch wood"? The Lady of the House and I sometimes do!

I like the texture and feel of wood; whether it is furniture, ornaments or an actual tree trunk. It always feels warm, and some wood, such as sandalwood, even has its own distinctive smell.

Fortunately, there have always been men and women who have taken up wood handicrafts and delighted each generation with their skills. "Touching wood" is something of a superstitious phrase, but it refers to touching the Cross, so is Christian in origin.

While there are trees growing, we will always be able to "touch wood", and remember the Carpenter of Nazareth.

THE FRIENDSHIP BOOK

THE noticeboard I saw outside a country church bore this message:

"The only Bible most people read is you!"

What did it mean? Surely you and I can't be likened to a book? But that Book contains the word of God, His standards and the doings of His people.

In our treatment of other folk in the workplace, the supermarket, on the sports field and amongst friends, we are often the only contact they may have with Christian ideals. We should all be walking Bibles!

I'D like to share these reflective words sent to me by Jean Harris of York:

Thank You
For the answer to my prayer;
Thank You
For showing me you care;
Thank You
For guidance on the way;
Thank You
For everything today.

WE all tend to take so much for granted — our friends, neighbours and the many possessions we have and enjoy. Our lives are much richer, with far more blessings than we usually admit.

I recently overheard this conversation:

"Have you sold your house yet?"

"No. After we read the estate agent's description, it seemed just the place we were looking for, so we decided to stay!"

THE FRIENDSHIP BOOK

THE architect Sir Edwin Lutyens is famous, yet his friend and partner Miss Gertrude Jekyll is scarcely remembered unless you happen to be a garden enthusiast.

When she was 50, her eyesight, which had always been poor, began to deteriorate. Threatened with blindness, she was advised to give up the painting and embroidery which meant so much to her, but being a determined lady, she decided to create her pictures by planting flowers instead.

As her sight grew worse, she found compensations in the heightening of her other senses — the ability to hear a hedgehog moving through the undergrowth; to distinguish plants by their scent as she brushed past them; and to identify a tree by the feel of its bark.

It was at this time that she met Lutyens, then a young architect at the beginning of his career and they struck up a friendship and most successful partnership, building fine houses and designing and planting the gardens to go with them, which lasted for more than 30 years.

After Gertrude Jekyll's death, Lutyens erected a memorial to his friend and partner in the churchyard where she was buried with the simplicity he knew she would have wanted:

GERTRUDE JEKYLL
ARTIST
GARDENER
CRAFTSWOMAN

AND the Lord shall be king over all the earth: in that day shall there be one Lord, and his name one.   Zechariah 14:9

THE FRIENDSHIP BOOK

I HEAR about the "good old days",
And venture to reflect
The basis of this well-worn phrase
Gains much in retrospect.

History often tends to be
Considerate and kind,
Throwing sympathetic light
On days left far behind.

When times were tough in many ways,
And wages were so low,
Were those indeed the "good old days"
In years so long ago?

While memories can take us back
To sparkling days of youth,
Sometimes this nostalgic track
Diverts us from the truth.

Although the "good old days" of yore
Are worthy of some praise,
I wish we heard a little more
About the "good NEW days"!
J.M. Robertson.

A T our local nursery school, children are expected to put on their own shoes by the time they are four years old.

Young Johnny, who had just reached that milestone in his life, was told to do this by his teacher. He did his best, only to be told that his shoes were on the wrong feet.

"But," he protested. "I haven't got any other feet!"

WEDNESDAY—FEBRUARY 10.

YEARS ago I heard a preacher say, "The stars are stupendous, but the little man looking through the telescope is even more wonderful." I have forgotten who the preacher was and I can't remember much about the rest of the sermon, but I think those words will remain with me for ever.

Size isn't everything. In this vast universe we may feel small and insignificant, but we can think, we can worship, we can love, we can help others. These things make us "big" in the true sense of the word. May that thought encourage us today.

THURSDAY—FEBRUARY 11.

ALL my life I've disliked prejudice. We're born under one sun, in one world. I wonder what the need is for some to feel superior to others?

Perhaps that wonderful comedian Groucho Marx had the right idea. Once he and his young son were stopped as they tried to enter an exclusive American Country Club. Jews, he was told, were not allowed to bathe there.

Groucho thought for a moment and then, "I'll tell you what," he said, "my son is only half-Jewish, so can he get wet up to his waist?"

Humour is the greatest antidote to life's prejudices.

FRIDAY—FEBRUARY 12.

ARE you looking for a good maxim to follow as you go through life? This quotation may provide you with the answer:

"When doing things for yourself, be guided by your head. When doing things for others, be guided by your heart."

THE FRIENDSHIP BOOK

BEING in a romantic mood thinking of St Valentine's Day tomorrow, I am remembering an old formula for that most satisfying occupation called matchmaking.

> *16 Looks make 1 Wink,*
> *16 Winks make 1 Smile,*
> *14 Smiles make 1 Nod,*
> *2 Nods make 1 Word,*
> *28 Words make 1 Moonlight Meeting,*
> *4 Moonlight Meetings make 1 Kiss,*
> *20 Kisses make 1 Match.*

Martin Luther expressed his thoughts about the results of matchmaking like this: "There is no more lovely, friendly and charming relationship, communion, or company than a good marriage."

JESUS said unto him. Thou shalt love the Lord thy God with all thy heart, and with all thy soul, and with all thy mind.

Matthew 22:37

> *I PUT my hand*
> *In the Hand of God,*
> *And firm and sound*
> *Was the path that I trod,*
> *Safely he led*
> *Through the hours of the night,*
> *Out of the darkness*
> *Into the light.*

Jean Harris.

TUESDAY—FEBRUARY 16.

I'M no politician, but here is a saying about electioneering that has a lot of truth in it:

"God is voting for us all the time. The devil is voting against us all the time. The way *we* vote carries the election!"

WEDNESDAY—FEBRUARY 17.

I HAVE always had a great admiration for the work done among the poor by Mother Teresa in India, much of it concerned with the welfare of orphaned and unwanted children. I'm sure it is from the heart that she put together this prayer which has a great deal to teach us:

Lord, when I am hungry — give me someone in need of food;

When I am thirsty, send me someone needing a drink;

When I am cold, send me someone to warm;

When I am grieved, offer me someone to console;

When my cross grows heavy, let me share another's cross, too;

When I am poor, lead me to someone in need;

When I have not time, give me someone I can help a little while;

When I am humiliated, let me have someone to praise;

When I am disheartened, send me someone to cheer;

When I need understanding, give me someone who needs mine;

When I need to be looked after, send me someone to care for;

When I think only of myself, draw my thoughts to another.

IT was a moment of decision for John McKay. The man who had started his working life as a shepherd lad and had worked long hours over the years to build up successful businesses, now at last had the ticket that would make a dream come true — a flight on Concorde.

Then he decided he wouldn't go. He couldn't bring himself to use it. Instead he raffled the ticket for £3500 for the benefit of Cancer Research.

John McKay and his wife Jean don't only give money to the cause dear to their hearts. They give untold amounts of time. The shepherds' crooks which John has made in his Dumfriesshire home have been purchased by customers all over the world.

I don't suppose anyone knows of all the work the McKays have done for Cancer Research. Just let me say that I have been told that in six years they raised over £25,000.

It's nice to know that, after all, John got his flight on Concorde. His family secretly clubbed together to buy the ticket. He could hardly refuse to use that one, could he?

I COULDN'T help chuckling at the story I heard about a man from the American Deep South who, after leading a dissolute life, began to go to church.

"I've given up sin, Parson," he told his minister one day.

"That's good," said the minister, "and are you going to pay all your debts as well?"

"Now, wait a minute," the man protested, "you ain't talking about religion now — you're talking about business!"

SATURDAY—FEBRUARY 20.

OUR friend Mary finds some fascinating ways of passing the time. One day she told me, "I've been doing sums!"

"Really?" I said.

"Yes," she went on, "but not ordinary sums with numbers. I've been doing them with words."

I scratched my head, bewildered.

"I've just done one with the word 'friendship'," she said with a smile. "Just think, you can multiply and divide with friendship. It improves happiness and reduces sadness by doubling our joy and dividing our grief."

Mary is a mathematical wizard!

SUNDAY—FEBRUARY 21.

BUT the Lord of hosts shall be exalted in judgement, and God that is holy shall be sanctified in righteousness.

Isaiah 5:16

MONDAY—FEBRUARY 22.

HERE is a message in verse from Jacqueline M. Brown of Hornchurch, Essex. I like it for the beauty of the words as much as for the thought it expresses:

You cannot climb high mountains
Before you've walked low ground,
And on the road to wisdom
No short cuts can be found.
Have courage in adversity,
You will not strive in vain;
There never was a rainbow
Without a fall of rain.

GIFT OF GOLD

THE FRIENDSHIP BOOK

MONEY is something we can't do without, but warnings abound, especially in the Scriptures, about the folly of coveting wealth. "Love of money is the root of all evil" is a lesson we learn early in life from wise parents and teachers.

"If you have enough to live on," our friend Albert says, "you don't have to worry about money. I reckon we should follow God's judgment."

"What's that?" I asked.

"Well, you can tell what God thinks of money," he smiled. "Just look at some of the people he gives it to!"

WHEN Helen Hayes, the actress, was young, she was told by a producer that she could probably become one of the great actresses of her time if only she were four inches taller. Some of her friends and fellow thespians tried to stretch and pull her, but despite their efforts and a lot of discomfort, she grew no taller. However, as a result of all the exercises, her posture became exceedingly straight and she became the tallest five-foot woman in the world!

So impressive did she look on stage that, despite the limitation of her height, she once played Mary, Queen of Scots, one of the tallest queens in history.

Helen Hayes succeeded because, like many others, she chose to "walk tall", concentrating on her strong points, and overcoming her weak ones.

A FRIEND sent me a cutting from a Sussex parish magazine recently, announcing what sounds like a little miracle: "In view of the popularity of the church ladies' annual outing, it has been decided to hold it twice a year."

FRIDAY—FEBRUARY 26.

> WHEN Friendship's blooming — tend it.
>   If Gloom's beginning — end it.
> A hand's for helping — lend it.
> A smile costs nothing — spend it.

SATURDAY—FEBRUARY 27.

IN a village church the Lady of the House and I visit, wealthy families lie in ornate tombs bearing Latin inscriptions describing their achievements and their generosity to the village. Outside, the worn headstones of the villagers record the simple lives of passing generations.

When we visited the church last month, there had been a funeral earlier that day. William Clover had died. We were told that the church had been packed for his funeral service. He had been a friend to everyone — nothing was too much trouble for him. Friends remembered how they had never turned to him in vain for help or comfort.

As he lay ill in hospital, he heard that four of the nurses had arranged a motor caravan holiday on the continent, but it had broken down at the last minute. He arranged that his own small caravan should be delivered to the nurses' home in time for them to go.

None of this will be recorded on his gravestone, and he left no vast fortune, but his priceless legacy to the many who mourn him is simply the gift of having known him — a goldmine, indeed.

SUNDAY—FEBRUARY 28.

AND he said, The things which are impossible with men are possible with God.

Luke 18:27

MARCH

NEAR to where friends live in the Lake District, there is a little old church, St Michael's, beside the river Derwent.

I have often visited it in Lent when there were no flowers inside, but it does not, in fact, need any — the light shining through the slits and lancets floods every clean-swept corner, and the stones in the Norman arch are brown, pale fawn and rose red. A card beside a window, left by Sir John Betjeman, reads: "A perfect English harmony of man and nature".

This is also true of the picture outside the church. The snowdrops are the first to appear under the old beech tree, followed by aconites and early crocuses. These are followed by daffodils — wild ones.

Now, miles away, in a busy town, in Springtime, I close my eyes and see St Michael's by the river, the snowdrops, crocuses and daffodils under that beech tree. I relax, and find again in memory the holiness and peace of beauty.

HERE'S a children's story, and since I found it in a church magazine it surely must be true!

Two small boys were on the way home from Sunday School, where they had been learning about the importance of saying their prayers. One of them was doubtful if his mother said her nightly prayers, but the other little chap was quite certain that his mother did.

"Oh, yes," he said, "my mummy prays every night. As soon as I go to bed, I hear her say, 'Thank God'!"

THE FRIENDSHIP BOOK

Here is a poem for Springtime written by Margaret Ingall:

SOFTLY Spring is coming, singing,
  Winging high and dipping low,
Heard in distant songbirds' calling,
  Whispered in the river's flow.
Echoed by the streams that tumble,
  Fallen blossom whirling by,
Floating on translucent ripples,
  Dancing under dappled sky.
Rustled in the boughs and branches,
  Murmured by the waking trees,
Purred among the pussy willows,
  Swaying, playing, in the breeze.
All the land is softly stirring,
  All alive to see and hear,
Clothed in all her rainbow colours,
  Spring is singing, winging near!

HAVE you ever wondered why little silver horseshoes are put on wedding cakes and why they are supposed to be lucky?

It is said that many years ago, St Dunstan, who was a blacksmith, was visited in his forge by the devil who asked for shoes to be fitted to his feet.

Dunstan recognised his visitor and so, while fixing horseshoes to the devil's feet, nailed the shoes to the wall to trap him. The devil tried desperately to free himself, but his efforts were in vain.

Before agreeing to release him, Dunstan made the devil promise that he would never enter a place where there was a horseshoe on the wall, or for that matter, it seems, on a cake!

FRIDAY—MARCH 5.

I HAVE just been reading an old book about prayer and came on this passage:

"Prayer is not just talking to God, not even simply listening to God. It is living with God. It is in prayer that we see things through God's eyes.

"We couldn't do better than to begin each day with the praise of His Name on our lips, and walk through each day knowing that we walk with Him, sure that He knows and will meet all our needs."

SATURDAY—MARCH 6.

I T was a beautiful Spring day so the Lady of the House suggested that we go for a walk in "our bluebell wood". It isn't really *our* wood, of course — it's a small spinney which is in the care of a local amenity body. Over the years, we have taken bluebell bulbs from our garden and planted them in clumps wherever there was a bare spot. Like many things in life, the beginning was quite insignificant, just a few flowers here and there. But the bulbs spread and now each year there is a carpet of blue beneath the trees which gives us immense pleasure — as we hope it does for many others who walk there.

All around us we can find opportunities to "plant" something worthwhile, to brighten somebody's day and help to leave our world a better place. Often the results can surprise even ourselves. After all, "tall oaks from little acorns grow".

SUNDAY—MARCH 7.

F OR Christ is the end of the law for righteousness to every one that believeth. Romans 10:4

THE FRIENDSHIP BOOK

WHEN we are growing older it is easy to sit back and live on memories of past achievements, but remember that it's never too late to try something new.

Tennyson wrote a poem on the subject:
Old age hath yet his honour and his toil;
Death closes all: but something ere the end,
Some work of noble note, may yet be done . . .

It goes on:
'Tis not too late to seek a newer world.

He was writing of Ulysses who, in his old age, invited his friends to set out with him on a new adventure!

Marie Tempest, the famous actress, was 65 when she was given a leading rôle in a play. She gave a marvellous performance, but the play itself was a failure. All was doom and gloom at the party held when the play was taken off, but Marie suddenly perked up and said quite seriously, "Everybody at the beginning of their career must expect reverses."

Yes, it's never too late . . .

TUESDAY—MARCH 9.

A CHURCH on the outskirts of a city had a huge banner on a notice board in the grounds bearing the following message:

"WHAT IS MISSING FROM
THIS CH . . CH?"

I puzzled over the meaning, before realising that the missing letters were "U" and "R" — "you are!"

What a clever way to get the message across! I hope it attracted a lot of interest and resulted in more people feeling the need to become involved in that church's work.

THE FRIENDSHIP BOOK

THERE'S something very special about getting up for an early morning walk on a clear bright morning with a promise of Spring in the air. To greet the day when the rest of the world is asleep and the only sounds are the singing of the birds and the few early travellers on their way to work, always gives me a feeling of contentment.

I am put in mind of something the author Derek Tangye wrote:

"A morning to be aware of one's own luck. A morning to shout one's gratitude to the heavens. A morning to sympathise with those on trains and buses crowding into cities, or those passing through factory gates to join the din of machinery. Here was peace. Here was the ultimate which man seeks . . . nothing that a millionaire could buy, nothing that greed or envy could win, equals the reward of a Spring morning."

Although the walk he was describing took place on a lonely Cornish cliff with a breathtaking view of the sea, I think we can all share something of the pleasure and gratitude he describes wherever we are at this time of the year.

HE sat there very comfortable,
Humming a little tune,
While I was busy at my chores,
He lazed all afternoon.
Now doesn't it seem unfair to you
That he should be doing that?
If I come back in another life,
I, too, must be a cat!

Phyllis Ellison.

THE FRIENDSHIP BOOK

AN enterprising fund-raising scheme that I heard of recently was launched by Tessa Twill, wife of the Archdeacon of Canterbury.

It all began in 1988 at the Lambeth Conference of Bishops from all over the world. Their wives, thrown into each other's company while their husbands were in conference, formed close friendships and were sad at the thought of losing touch when it was all over. So at the end of the conference, Tessa suggested that they should all exchange recipes from their own part of the world which would be a shared interest and a means of continuing the links that had been made.

At the back of her mind, too, was an idea for raising money for the Church Urban Fund. This was the scheme started by Dr Robert Runcie, when Archbishop of Canterbury, to finance projects to help the underprivileged in the inner cities, regardless of colour, age, sex or religion.

The recipes rolled in from around the world and were compiled as "The Bishops' Cook Book". Some of the material was incorporated on "Bishops' Tea Towels" designed in ecclesiastical colours such as cardinal red and episcopal purple.

The items went on sale in due course. Profit from the enterprise was £26,000 which was considerable from an outlay of only £300. But then, as it was said, "You can't put a price on goodwill, dedicated volunteers and a huge dose of Christian caring".

A VISITOR was taken aback when her hostess told her, "I always feel better after you've gone."

I hope what she really meant was, "I always feel better after you've been!"

SUNDAY—MARCH 14.

FOR God is the King of all the earth: sing ye praises with understanding.

Psalms 47:7

MONDAY—MARCH 15.

I LIKE the story of the father who was telling his little son about his war-time exploits and experiences — and a fine story he made of it all!

When he had finished, the small boy asked innocently, "Daddy, what were all the other soldiers for?"

TUESDAY—MARCH 16.

HAVE you heard of the Holy Shadow? A saint long ago was said to be so good that the angels came down to see how a mortal man could possibly be so godly. He went about his daily work spreading virtue as readily as a star sheds light or a flower emits perfume, without being aware of it.

The angels offered him other gifts, perhaps the gift of miracles, the ability to heal the sick, or convert folk. He refused them, saying he simply asked that God would give him grace so that "I may do a great deal of good without ever knowing it."

So the angels arranged that every time the saint's shadow fell where he couldn't see it, it should have a healing effect — making withered plants grow again, giving joy to the sorrowful, and restoring health to the sick. The un-named saint was never even aware of the blessings that flowed from him.

That is why he came to be known as the Holy Shadow, a lovely name for a humble and truly good man.

THE FRIENDSHIP BOOK

MY friend Barbara Jemison of Bridlington sent me these cheerful lines:

> In spite of all you read about
>   The greedy human race,
> I sometimes feel this bad old world's
>   A very friendly place.
> The rank and file can't be too bad
>   For if I chance to be
> Out shopping, and I smile at folk,
>   They all smile back at me.

A BURST of warm Spring weather early in the year had brought fast growth to some of my garden shrubs, and it seemed as if there would be a fine display before very long. But alas, there came a night of very severe frost and when I went out to inspect my plants, I was dismayed by the damage.

Hopefully, the clematis will keep its buds, while the buddleia and fuchsias can be cut back and will flower later on, but the hydrangeas will bear no flowers this season and may have been killed off altogether.

It's rather like life, isn't it? A good relationship can be marred by a sudden unkind word or thoughtless act. Often, the relationship is strong enough for the hurt to be repaired, but sometimes it leaves a wound that is difficult to heal. It is wise to heed the old warning, "Least said — soonest mended".

More than 200 years ago Isaac Watts wrote these lines:

> I'll not willingly offend
>   Nor be easily offended.
> What's amiss I'll strive to mend,
>   And endure what can't be mended.

LOOKING TO THE FUTURE

FRIDAY—MARCH 19.

A FRIEND was telling a Quaker all about the financial troubles one of his poor relations had gone through. "I felt really sorry for him," he said sadly.

I like the old Quaker's reply, "Yes, but did you feel sorry in the right place — in your pocket?"

SATURDAY—MARCH 20.

MOTHERING SUNDAY falls on the fourth Sunday in Lent. Years ago, it was the day when people were allowed a break in the strict period of fasting and young members of the family who were in service, came home, bringing nosegays of wild flowers for their mothers. Tea usually included a piece of traditional simnel cake.

Today it has become more commercialised, but nothing takes away from the desire to express in gifts or loving acts all that a mother's care has meant to us. Making a home is one of the greatest God-given tasks there is, and one of the most demanding. William Barclay expressed it beautifully in a prayer for mothers:

"Help me to remember this when I am tired of making beds, and washing clothes, and cleaning floors, and mending clothes, and standing in shops . . . Help me to make this home such that the family will always be eager to come back to it, and such that, when the children grow up and go out to their own homes, they will have nothing but happy memories of the home from which they have come."

So I raise my hat to the day's most important people — mothers!

D

THE FRIENDSHIP BOOK

BLESSED be the Lord God of Israel for ever and ever. And all the people said, Amen, and praised the Lord.

Chronicles I 16:36

*B*USY *people always seem*
The ones who understand
Someone else's problems,
And find time to lend a hand;
Yes, we all have problems,
But life has often shown,
By overcoming others' woes,
We overcome our own.

Elizabeth Gozney.

HAVE you ever dialled a telephone number, got a crossed line, and found yourself listening to a conversation between two people who are complete strangers to you?

It can be frustrating, especially if your call is urgent. I usually replace the receiver and try again later. If this fails, I report a fault on the line to the operator.

Sometimes we get crossed lines with people, too. We may have misheard what someone was trying to tell us or we put a wrong interpretation on their words. However, once we realise what has happened, it is easy to sort things out and restore the lines of communication again. What a happy day that is!

THE FRIENDSHIP BOOK

WHEN he was very young, nobody knew why David had learning difficulties. When he was six, his mother was told that he would never amount to much. Concentrate on your two younger sons, she was told.

Of course, being a mother, she concentrated on all three, each one receiving encouragement and equal amounts of love and attention. Each blossomed in his own way.

The younger two worked hard, gained places at university, and when they qualified, their mother's heart was full of pride.

But what about David? Well, a more fulfilled and happy young man you would never meet. He works as a shelf filler in a large supermarket where his helpful manner and cheerful smile endear him to both staff and customers. He and several other handicapped youngsters have just gained their Duke of Edinburgh Bronze awards. David is also a member of a hiking club and enjoys country rambles and hill walking.

Not amount to much indeed! David has literally climbed mountains.

THE other day I had a letter from my friend Maurice in the Devonshire town of Bideford. He told me that a few days earlier in Northam Square, the engine of a car driven by a young lady had broken down.

Traffic soon built up and the young man in the car behind started sounding his horn. The lady got out and said to him: "I've just had a good idea. You try to get my car started, and I'll sit in yours and blow your horn!"

FRIDAY—MARCH 26.

A LADY at a writers' group meeting was reading her piece of prose, when she was asked to read louder because her voice was too faint.

With that, she pulled her hearing aid out of her ear and said, "*I* can't hear myself with that thing in, either!"

SATURDAY—MARCH 27.

A PAMPHLET plopped through our letterbox, headed The Polite Society. Immediately, I was reminded of my Scouting days when one of the basic laws was (it still is): "A Scout (and Guide) is Polite and Courteous."

The founder of the Scout and Guide Movement, Lord Baden-Powell, knew how important it was to be polite and considerate to our fellow men. How much he would have approved of this new Society, founded in 1986, which seeks to restore the values of good manners, and of thought for others.

An American once said to a Frenchman who had been behaving courteously towards him, "What's the use of all this politeness? There's nothing in it — it's only wind."

The Frenchman replied, "There's nothing but wind in a tyre, but it gets you over the jolts of the road very comfortably."

How true — manners maketh the man, indeed!

SUNDAY—MARCH 28.

A NOTHER parable put he forth unto them, saying, The kingdom of heaven is likened unto a man which sowed good seed in his field.

Matthew 13:24

A PLACE TO PONDER

THE FRIENDSHIP BOOK

ONE fine Spring afternoon the Lady of the House decided to leave the washing-up and go for a stroll with me while the sun was still shining.

People had already been busy in their gardens — lawns were neatly cut and borders tidied to show off the colourful tulips, wallflowers and primulas. Farther on we could see that the avenue of cherry trees planted by the Civic Society was showing a cloud of fairy pink blossom, and here and there on corners and verges, clumps of daffodils were nodding their heads, brightening the view for all who passed.

There was so much to delight our eyes — all thoughtfully provided for us by others — and for a moment or two we sat on our favourite seat to admire it all. I was put in mind of something St Francis of Assisi said: "He who works with his hands is a labourer. He who works with his hands and his head is a craftsman. He who works with his hands and his head and his heart is an artist."

I MET my young friend Billy today.
"Mr Gay," he asked, "what is grey, has four legs and a trunk?"

"That's an easy one, Billy," I replied. "It's an elephant!"

"Wrong," chuckled the young rascal. "It's a mouse going on holiday!"

ONE of my colleagues spotted an amusing sign outside a second-hand shop. It read: "We buy rubbish; we sell antiques".

 APRIL

THURSDAY—APRIL 1.

*H*OW like my life are April days
    With sunshine and with rain —
A bright blue sky, a sudden storm,
    Then warmth and light again.
God guide me in the gloom and give
    Me wit to find each day
The flowers, which both the rain and sun,
    Bring out to cheer my way.

Barbara Jemison.

FRIDAY—APRIL 2.

MANY people find it hard to accept the prospect of old age. Shakespeare somewhat cynically described it as "sans teeth, sans eyes, sans taste, sans everything." Yet there are many compensations in growing older — a less hurried lifestyle, time to indulge in pastimes we previously haven't had time for, and, hopefully, a growth in wisdom, tolerance and serenity.

I like the view of author Henry Durbanville, who wrote, "I feel so sorry for folks who don't like to grow old. I revel in my years. They enrich me. If God should say to me, 'I will let you begin over again and you may have your youth back once more,' I should say, 'If You don't mind, I prefer to go on growing old.' I would not exchange the peace of mind, the abiding rest of soul, the measure of wisdom I have gained from the sweet and bitter and perplexing experiences of life . . . My 'outward man' is perishing, but my 'inward man' is being joyously renewed day by day."

That's the spirit!

SATURDAY—APRIL 3.

IF you look back with nostalgia at seaside donkey rides, you will no doubt be in sympathy with the aims of the Donkey Sanctuary at Sidmouth in Devon which has cared for countless donkeys fallen on hard times.

The Sanctuary was started by Elizabeth Fenton who realised that while there were organisations to look after horses, dogs and cats, there was little done for donkeys which were often badly abused, although they are such a help to man. So she opened the sanctuary where sick and tired donkeys are taken in, given medical care, comfortable quarters, lots of love, and are safe for the rest of their lives. In addition, she has gone round the world opening clinics and tending donkeys to increase their life span for their desperately poor owners.

From early times, donkeys have been used as beasts of burden and, as we approach Palm Sunday, we remember that it was a donkey that carried Christ on his triumphal entry into Jerusalem. From that day, it is said, donkeys have carried the mark of a cross on their back.

SUNDAY—APRIL 4.

FATHER, glorify thy name. Then came there a voice from heaven, saying, I have both glorified it, and will glorify it again.

John 12:28

MONDAY—APRIL 5.

I DON'T know who D.S. Jordan was, but I like his three-fold *bon mot:*

"Wisdom is knowing what to do next; skill, how to do it; and virtue, doing it."

THE FRIENDSHIP BOOK

THE Lady of the House and I often visit a park with a beautifully-kept rose garden, and we have got to know Fred, the man who cares for it. One day he was busy pruning the roses. The Lady of the House watched and asked him exactly what he was doing. "Well, I always cut away the inward-looking small branches first," he said. "If you do this you will always get a fine bloom, as the flowers will face outwards, ready to receive the sun."

So, if you ever think you're becoming "inward-looking", that feeling which prevents you from becoming creative and taking an interest in life outwith your immediate horizons, take Fred's advice — prune away selfish thoughts, think of others — and look for the rays of sunlight which will break through. You'll find that the rewards are well worth the initial effort.

THE name Lewis Carroll immediately reminds us of his marvellous children's book, "Alice In Wonderland". It is easy to forget that the man who created that wonderful fantasy world was, by profession, a mathematics lecturer. When "Alice" appeared, it was extremely popular. Queen Victoria read it and was so entranced that she invited the author to the palace for a chat.

Before he left, she told him that she would be very honoured if she could be the first person to receive a copy of his next book.

Great was her excitement when, some time later, a parcel arrived from him. Another fascinating adventure story? Alas, no. It was a book on a very abstruse form of mathematics!

THURSDAY—APRIL 8.

I WAS looking out the window at our garden one morning, and saw a female blackbird searching for material to build her nest. She picked up dried stalks of hollyhocks and small pieces of bark and grass cuttings in her beak. I was surprised how much she was able to carry at one time.

I watched as she made several more trips over the lawn. Meanwhile, the male blackbird was hunting nearby for worms, but his mate wasn't distracted by him at all. I was impressed by her diligence and single-mindedness. She spent a long time finding exactly the right kind of materials to make her nest secure.

How easy it is for us when faced with a daunting task to be distracted and, as a result, not do a thorough job, or even put off the task altogether until another day or another week.

Instinct told our blackbird that she must finish the work before egg-laying and family-rearing could begin.

FRIDAY—APRIL 9.

I CAN never resist browsing round the white elephant stall whenever our Scouts hold their rummage sale. As the saying goes, "One man's rubbish is another man's treasure".

Amongst the assortment of bric-à-brac, odd plates, pictures and presents from the seaside, I picked up a wall plaque. It was chipped and crazed, but the verse on it was still clear enough:

> *The tongue can be a blessing,*
> *Or the tongue can be a curse;*
> *Say, friend, how are you using yours,*
> *For better, or for worse?*

SATURDAY—APRIL 10.

AS I was reading the background to the origins of simnel cake I was reminded how children used to leave home at a very early age to work as domestic servants or trades apprentices. By the 17th century, they were often given a holiday on Mothering Sunday so that they could visit their families. They would take gifts of flowers or simnel cakes.

There are many stories telling how this cake got its name. One is that a brother and sister wanted to make a cake for their mother, and argued about the way to cook it. One wanted to bake it, and the other to boil it. In the end, they made a boiled cake and a baked cake and placed the two together. The cake was called simnel from their names — Simon and Nell!

The more likely reason for the name, is that the cake was made with a fine flour called "simila". The main thing is that we now associate this delicious treat with Easter — a time for loving and giving.

SUNDAY—APRIL 11.

AND when they found not his body, they came, saying, that they had also seen a vision of angels, which said that he was alive.

Luke 24:23

MONDAY—APRIL 12.

I LIKE this old saying which has been passed on to me:

"The perfect wife is one who doesn't expect a perfect husband."

When I showed it to the Lady of the House she smiled, but said nothing. A little later she commented quietly, "There must be a lot of perfect wives about!"

GOLDEN GIRL

THE FRIENDSHIP BOOK

I HAVE been reading the story about a church in America which was celebrating a special occasion with a reunion between past and present members. One man was a millionaire and he told the assembled congregation of an incident in his childhood.

He had earned his first dollar for some small job and was considering all the different ways he might use it. Then he heard a missionary speaker who talked about the urgent need for money to support work in the mission field. The boy had to decide whether to give up his precious dollar or not.

"The Lord won," said the man proudly, "and I am convinced that the reason God has blessed me so much is that when I was a boy I gave him, that day, everything I had."

Everybody was most impressed by his story until a little old lady in the front row piped up, "And I dare you to do it again!"

THERE'S a clematis in our garden — that is, when we are able to find it! In Spring, on the fence where it grows, there is a mass of green leaves all entwined. These leaves belong to a honeysuckle, a climbing rose and the clematis.

The clematis is one of those plants that needs another plant for support, and it is only when the purple flowers appear that we are able to see it clearly.

Have you found, as I have, that when you need support in a crisis, say, during a serious illness or other misfortune, if that support is given readily by friends and family, then it enables us to hold up our heads and show our true colours — exactly like our clematis?

THE FRIENDSHIP BOOK

THE British are a nation of dog lovers — indeed, many keen dog owners claim their pets are almost human and capable of speech. This "Dog's Prayer" appeared in a friend's church magazine:

"O Lord of all creatures, grant that man, my master, may be as faithful to other men as I am to him. Make him as loving towards his family and friends as I am loving to him. Grant that he may guard with honesty the good things with which thou hast endowed him as honestly as I guard his.

"Give him, O Lord, a happy and ready smile, as happy and spontaneous as the wagging of my tail. Make him as ready to show gratitude as I am eager to lick his hand. Give him patience as great as mine when I await his return without complaining. Grant him my courage and my readiness to sacrifice all for him, even my own life. May he possess my youthful spirit and joy of thought.

"O Lord of all creatures, as I am in truth only a dog, may my master always be truly a man."

HUMAN nature never changes, does it? I had a chuckle at this old verse that the Lady of the House came across recently:

There was a sign upon a wall,
And that sign said "Wet Paint",
And every mortal that passed by—
A Sinner or a Saint,
Put out a finger, touched the wall
And then they onward sped,
And as they wiped their fingertips,
"They're right — it is!" they said.

THE FRIENDSHIP BOOK

A FRIEND has been attending a self-help group. Part of the therapy, he told me, has been that each week at the beginning of the session, members are asked to talk about something they have felt thankful for since they last met. It could have been a lovely surprise gift or a night at the theatre; on the other hand it might be something we are inclined to regard as quite ordinary — a good night's sleep, a sunny day, an encouraging telephone call or an unexpected bunch of flowers.

The point of the exercise, as my friend had discovered, was to focus minds on the many good and positive things in our lives that we are sometimes inclined to take for granted.

This story made me aware of all the things *I* have to be thankful for and I am going to put the exercise into practice, starting today. Will you join me?

F OR the kingdom of God is not meat and drink; but righteousness, and peace, and joy in the Holy Ghost.

Romans 14:17

T HE Lady of the House was smiling to herself on her return home from a shopping trip. The greengrocer, a jovial character, had been vigorously extolling the health-giving properties of his produce, especially carrots, which, he swore, would help his customers to see in the dark.

"Well," he challenged them, "have you ever seen a rabbit wearing glasses?"

TUESDAY—APRIL 20.

MY dictionary defines love as an intense emotion of affection, warmth, fondness and regard towards a person. In fact, love is not just a passive feeling, but something very active working on behalf of someone's good.

In his letter about love, St Paul tells us that "love is patient, love is kind. It does not envy, it does not boast, it is not proud. It is not rude, it is not self-seeking, it is not easily angered, it keeps no record of wrongs". Quite a lot to live up to!

When Wordsworth wrote "Lines Written Above Tintern Abbey", he spoke of "that best portion of a good man's life, his little, nameless, unremembered acts of kindness and of love", whilst more recently George Washington Carver, the American agriculturalist, summed it up neatly in these thoughtful lines:

> Be tender with the young,
> Compassionate with the aged,
> Sympathetic with the striving,
> And tolerant of the weak and strong.
> Indeed, at some time in our own lives,
> We could be all of these.

WEDNESDAY—APRIL 21.

HOW we strive for success! I suppose it is an instinctive urge in most people, yet before we let it completely dominate our lives we would be well advised to reflect on the pithy comment made by that great writer George Bernard Shaw:

"I dread success. To have succeeded is to have finished one's business on earth. I like a state of continual becoming, with a goal in front and not behind."

D

SECRET GLADE

THE FRIENDSHIP BOOK

THE standard rule with chain letters is to throw them in the bin and forget about them. However, I was told of a light-hearted one the other day which made me smile. It read:

"If you are unhappy with your vicar, simply ask your churchwarden to send a copy of this letter to six other churches who are also tired of their vicar. Then bundle up your vicar and send him to the church at the top of the list. Within a week you will receive 16,435 vicars — and one of them should be all right!"

EVELYN GLENNIE grew up on a farm near Aberdeen, and attended the local school. She is now a young woman, beautiful and full of vitality, especially where her work is concerned — she is, of course, a well-known musician who travels around the world.

When she was 12, she became completely deaf. Her family and teachers wondered what she would do with her life. She had no doubts. She told her careers adviser that she was going to be a musician.

"You can't play music if you are deaf," was the reply.

"You're not me, I know what I can do," she retorted indignantly. She has been as good as her word and plays percussion instruments to perfection.

At The Royal College of Music she learned that there is feedback of sound and rhythm through the body from percussion instruments, and was taught the technique of placing her hands on a wall where she can feel the vibrations of the notes.

I have heard courageous Evelyn play solo and also accompanied by an orchestra. Her music is magical, for she plays straight from the heart.

THE FRIENDSHIP BOOK

A LITTLE luck, a little pluck,
In moments so demanding;
A little hope, a little scope
For help and understanding.
A little grit, a little bit
Of tact and toleration;
A little piece of each can cease
A lot of aggravation.

J.M. Robertson.

AND he shewed me a pure river of water of life, clear as crystal, proceeding out of the throne of God and of the Lamb.

Revelation 22:1

ONE of the regular features of a popular magazine is a page of funny stories with the heading "Laughter the Best Medicine". It proves that tonics need not come in the form of a doctor's prescription — a lot depends on your state of mind. Natural alternatives to accepted medicinal treatment are not just a modern suggestion.

St Aelred of Rievaulx had this to say in the Middle Ages:

"No medicine is more valuable, none more efficacious, none better suited to the cure of our temporal ills than a friend to whom we may turn for consolation in time of trouble — and with whom we may share our happiness in times of joy."

APRIL MORN

THE FRIENDSHIP BOOK

HERE are a few hints for gardeners that were once written for a church magazine by a minister:

Sow five rows of *PEAS*.
*P*resence at Church.
*P*atience.   *P*reparedness.
*P*romptness.
*P*erseverance.

Sow three rows of *LETTUCE*.
Let us be faithful to duty.
Let us be loyal and unselfish.
Let us love one another.

At any time of the year sow *TURNIPS*.
Turn up for meetings.
Turn up for new ideas.
Turn up with a smile.
Turn up with determination, to make everything
    good and worthwhile.

In hot weather develop our own *SQUASH*.
Squash gossip.
Squash criticism.
Squash indifference.
So make everything in the garden *LOVELY*.

Wise words for us to ponder over today.

THE other day I came across this homespun philosophy: "If there is anywhere on your horizon a spot of light, fix your eyes upon it, and turn your thoughts away from the clouds which may cover the rest of the sky. One spot of blue is worth a skyful of grey."

THE FRIENDSHIP BOOK

ST COLUMBA was born in Ireland about 50 years after the death of St Patrick. His parents had been converted to Christianity and Columba became a monk. When he was about 40, civil war broke out, and Columba decided to leave his homeland for ever. Taking 12 friends with him, he set sail for Scotland and landed on Iona, that peaceful island with clear sea water and white sandy beaches.

He set up a monastic community and travelled to the mainland preaching the gospel and training men as priests to carry on his work. By the time he died in 597, a Church had been established in Scotland.

After the Reformation the abbey fell into ruins, and it was not until the 20th century that the work of restoration began under the guidance of a Church of Scotland minister. By 1960 the work was completed and the Iona Community was born, a group of about 200 people committed to a simple way of life, trying to capture the essence of Celtic Christianity.

Today, many seek the special peace that is to be found there and all are welcome to share in the common life of worship, work and recreation. Here is one of the lovely prayers from the Community:

O God our Creator,
Your kindness has brought us the gift of a new day.
Help us to leave yesterday
And not to covet tomorrow,
But to accept the uniqueness of today.

DO not throw cold water
On someone else's schemes;
Throw instead a lifeline,
To help them with their dreams.

Anne Kreer.

MAY

SATURDAY—MAY 1.

A CLERGYMAN friend has been telling me of the great variety of excuses people make for not going to church. "But that's not all," he chuckled. "I get excuses for other things as well. Once when I was preaching I looked down from the pulpit and saw that one of my churchwardens had his eyes closed and seemed to have nodded off. When I spoke to him about this after the service, he just chuckled and said, 'I had my eyes closed because I was praying that your helpful sermon wouldn't fall on deaf ears!' "

SUNDAY—MAY 2.

HE that hath received his testimony hath set to his seal that God is true.   John 3:33

MONDAY—MAY 3.

IT was early Sunday morning. The sun was shining and I thought I was the only person in the park. Then I saw an elderly lady picking up things from the grass. She was collecting discarded bottles and cans in a cardboard box.

She saw me looking and smiled. "I come here every Sunday," she explained. "A lot of people have picnics on Saturday and some — well, they're not very tidy, are they?"

I agreed. "But don't you feel angry that you should be having to clean up after them?"

"Sometimes I do," she said. "But that never lasts long, and mostly I just wish that another 10 people would come and join me."

So, after that, what could I do but lend a hand and help to fill her box!

LAZY AFTERNOON

TUESDAY—MAY 4.

THE LADY OF THE HOUSE has a number of good friends, and among those who call in now and then for a chat are two I am thinking of particularly. Whenever I see one of these ladies coming up the garden path, I give a little sigh, for I know her visit will be one long catalogue of grumbles about the way life has treated her.

On the other hand, I am always pleased to see the other lady arrive, for although she has had much experience of the knocks and hardships of life, she is always cheerful and looks on the positive side.

There's a lot of truth in the saying "what you look for is what you get". Centuries ago, somebody wrote on the wall of a cell in the Tower of London: "The most unhappy man is he that is not patient in adversity. For men are not killed with the adversities they have, but with the impatience they suffer".

I am reminded, too, of the bed-ridden lady who said, "I admit this is not one of my best days, but the lower I am in bed, the more I can see of the blue sky."

WEDNESDAY—MAY 5.

BARBARA JEMISON sent me these verses she copied from an old scrapbook:

White clouds in a clear blue sky,
Gardens fresh and fair,
Sunny mornings, golden noons,
Birdsong everywhere.

Nods and smiles from pleasant folk,
Children sing and shout,
What a lot of things there are
To be glad about!

THE FRIENDSHIP BOOK

OBERAMMERGAU is more than just a pretty village in the mountains of Bavaria. In 1633 the villagers were struck by the plague that was then devastating Europe. They prayed for deliverance, and when the miracle happened they vowed that every ten years they would enact the Passion of Christ and his Resurrection and Ascension as an everlasting thanksgiving. The only year they failed to keep their promise was in 1940, during the Last War.

Almost the whole village is involved in the day-long acted scenes, the choir or orchestra, or in acting as hosts to the endless streams of visitors. Everything is authentic. No make-up is permitted, beards must be real and the everyday lives of those taking part must be able to bear scrutiny.

There's a memorable story about the 1930 production. A group of tourists were standing around watching a rehearsal, then afterwards one of them asked if he might hold the cross for a moment so that his wife could take a photograph of him bearing it. It was agreed, but the man staggered under its weight.

"It's real!" he gasped.

"Of course it's real," replied the man taking the rôle of Jesus. "If I can't carry His cross, how can I play the part?"

IN his great book, "The Brothers Karamazov", Dostoyevsky has this striking passage:

"Love all God's creation, the whole and every grain of sand in it. Love every leaf, every ray of God's light. Love the animals, love the plants, love everything. If you love everything, you will perceive the divine mystery in things."

THE FRIENDSHIP BOOK

CATCH ONE IF YOU CAN

IF someone sold smiles,
I'd be first on the spot,
I'd spend all my money.
I'd buy all the lot.
Then when the wind blew,
I'd toss them away,
Hoping others would catch them,
To brighten their day.
Phyllis Ellison.

REJOICE in the Lord alway: and again I say, Rejoice.

Philippians 4:4

WHEN my cousin Peter was a child brimming over with the latest plans, and always eager for the immediate arrival of the exciting things in life such as holidays, birthdays and Christmas, he would ask his mother about outings or presents, and she would always reply, "All being well and God willing."

Somehow, these words always seemed to cast a shadow on future plans. "How could things not be well?" a young child might ask. However, the true meaning of that phrase has become clear as the years have gone by. Our lives can indeed alter completely from hour to hour, and day to day.

I may not say "all being well and God willing" out aloud, but, I often think this apt phrase quietly to myself at the beginning and end of a day.

THE FRIENDSHIP BOOK

MY neighbour George is a keen beekeeper, and when I called round to buy some of his delicious honey, I found him tending his hives.

"Busy bee" is a well-known expression, and it comes directly from the social organisation of these insects. In the hive, each caste of bee has its own special function and works diligently for the benefit of the whole community. In fact, one band of workers flaps their wings at the entrance of the hive just to keep it cool!

I remember reading that Sir Christopher Wren was so impressed with the harmony to be found within a beehive that he designed many of his churches with domes as a symbol of harmony.

So, as I sit down to enjoy my toast and honey, I shall spare time to be grateful to the bees — and to all those on whom I depend to make life run sweetly and smoothly.

JOHN, a history teacher and archaeologist, came to live near us four years ago when he retired. He is a reserved man of few words who, not surprisingly, joined the local archaeological society. On one occasion when an eminent lecturer from Oxford University could not speak, John was asked at the last minute if he would fill the gap. Without notes, or any preparation, he enthralled his audience with his impromptu talk.

So now quiet John has become well-known in the district, and is frequently invited to speak to groups of all kinds. A man can be made to feel a substitute in life, but many great things have been done by so-called second-choice folk.

A KING once had a beautiful diamond. It was large and rare and he was very proud of it. One day, the diamond was scratched and became so disfigured that none of the court jewellers would risk trying to remove the mark. The king became very unhappy.

Not long afterwards, a new young jeweller came to court. He examined the diamond carefully and promised that he could make it even better than before. The king was very sceptical, but he decided to give the man a chance, so he handed over the diamond. When it was returned to him, the king was amazed, for the craftsman had engraved a beautiful rosebud around the flaw, and the ugly scratch had become the stem. It was, indeed, more beautiful than it was.

Sometimes we are all apt to think that something — a plan or a relationship — has been ruined. Instead of giving it up as a bad job, it's always worth taking another look. So often there *is* a way, not only of saving the situation, but of making it even better than before.

I T was so nice to see them in the supermarket. She was standing with her shopping trolley at one of the shelves. He was scanning the other shoppers until he saw her and then walked quickly over, put an arm round her shoulder and gave her an affectionate peck on the cheek.

Were they a couple of newly-weds still feeling starry-eyed? No, they were a couple of young-at-heart senior citizens just glad to be together again. After all, they had been parted a whole five minutes!

THE FRIENDSHIP BOOK

A SMALL boy was met by his mother after school and, as they walked home together, he told her, "We were talking to God in school today."

"Were you?" replied his mother. "And what had He to say to you?"

Her son thought for a moment and then replied, "Oh, well, *I* did most of the talking!"

It's maybe a fault some of the rest of us have, too!

A ND ye shall know that I am in the midst of Israel, and that I am the Lord your God, and none else: and my people shall never be ashamed.

Joel 2:27

A S Christian Aid week comes round once more, I am reminded of this story.

An old lady of 90 had made a difficult bus journey across the city of Belfast so that she could present her donation of £30 in person to the Christian Aid office. She said that the donation would have been larger, but she had lost her purse. The following week, she was back again. The missing purse had turned up in a drawer, so she had made another journey to hand over another £20.

"Since I had lost this money and found it again," she said, "I decided it was not for me."

Writing in the Christian Aid newspaper, Bishop Bill Flagg said, "The fact is that you can give money without loving, but you can never love without giving much more than money. Loving starts at home, but its infectiousness can never be contained."

THE FRIENDSHIP BOOK

I WAS sent this lovely prayer, and the friend who sent it tells me it was very special to a lady who died aged 101. Although she had been blind for many years, she was well known for her sweetness of character and her faith which never faltered:

Be with me, God, when I am glad and all my skies are blue,
And never let me fail to give my gratitude to you.
Be with me when the night is dark and shadows cross my heart
That I may always keep the faith and never grow apart.
Be with me, God, when I am home or when I travel far,
And help me to appreciate the beauty of a star.
Let not my heart be lonely or my footsteps go astray,
But teach me how to live my life according to your way.
Be with me, Father, everywhere in happiness and tears,
Be with me, God, and grant me grace through these last remaining years.

G. K. CHESTERTON could express great truths in a few elegant words. I felt I had to copy down these lines of his when I read them:

"Loving means to love the unlovable, or it is no virtue at all; forgiving means to pardon the unpardonable, or it is no virtue at all; faith means believing the unbelievable, or it is no virtue at all; and to hope means hoping when things are hopeless, or it is no virtue at all".

An elegant summing up of the road to perfection.

E

THE FRIENDSHIP BOOK

IT was our Sunday School Anniversary last week and it was good to see all our bright-faced youngsters singing, performing a play and collecting their prizes for regular attendance.

Our visiting preacher told an old story, but fresh, I fancy, to a new generation of children — the one about the little steam engine going steadily uphill and finding it hard work. As the climb got steeper, it chugged away to itself, "I think I can, I think I can, I think I can." Then, at long last, it reached the top and with a cheery whistle, it hurried down the other side saying, "I thought I could, I thought I could, I thought I could."

The moral the minister was pointing out was that it is easy to get discouraged in the attempt to master new things, or even to leave unfinished something we have already started, but determination and perseverance can overcome almost any situation.

In conclusion, he held up a card with IMPOSSIBLE written in large red letters. "This is something you will find in the dictionary," he said. "Leave it there!"

A LADY called Olive stays in our village. She's 82 years young and her door is always open to numerous family and friends who regularly visit her. Her telephone never stops ringing and requests for help never go unanswered. Nothing is too much trouble.

One day, I asked Olive how it was that she had so many friends. Her answer was very simple: "To have friends you have to *be* a friend."

Words of wisdom indeed.

THE FRIENDSHIP BOOK

AN unusual friendship between a man and his gardener resulted in the creation of one of our greatest and most beautiful gardens, Chatsworth Park, in Derbyshire, famous for its arboretum, extravagantly filled glasshouses and the Emperor Fountain which plays more than 200 feet into the air.

Joseph Paxton was born in 1801 to very poor parents, but it was evident that he had exceptional talents. Whilst working at the Horticultural Society's experimental garden at Chiswick, he met the 6th Duke of Devonshire who, recognising Paxton's ability, offered to make him the head gardener at Chatsworth. A cottage went with the job, which was fortunate for, soon after his arrival, he fell in love and married.

For over 30 years Paxton lived at Chatsworth working on the estate, and although he was once offered the job of head gardener at Windsor Castle for a salary of £1,000, he declined it. He was the Duke's adviser and constant companion. "To me he was a friend, if ever a man had one," wrote the Duke.

When the Duke died, Paxton retired from Chatsworth. He, too, died, soon afterwards, after doing what he loved doing most — attending a flower show. Even in death the two friends remained close, for they are buried in the same churchyard at Edensor near Chatsworth where they had been together for so much of their lives.

FOR I am not ashamed of the gospel of Christ: for it is the power of God unto salvation to every one that believeth; to the Jew first, and also to the Greek.

Romans 1:16

THE FRIENDSHIP BOOK

FOR many of us the sea holds mystery, even fear. Fortunately there are those for whom it holds no terror, only respect. I like the story of the pilot who came aboard to guide a large tanker into harbour. The captain asked him worriedly if he was sure he knew where all the rocks were.

"No," the pilot replied, "but I know where there aren't any."

If you know what to avoid in life, you will always stay in safe waters.

WHEN I do something right, nobody ever remembers it;
When I do something wrong, nobody ever forgets it.

That was the plaintive caption on the comical card sent to us by one of our young neighbours when she was on holiday.

Though I had to smile, I sympathised with the sentiment it expressed. It's the easiest thing in the world to grumble and find fault with other people, but it's a bad habit to get into. There's good and bad in all of us and if we are constantly criticising other people, we can so easily miss the good things about them — and then we are the loser, for it can make us disgruntled and disagreeable.

A very down-to-earth friend put it in a nutshell the other day when he said, "I have a very good wife — with a lot of faults. And she has a very good husband — with a lot of faults!"

As Thomas à Kempis wrote in the 15th century: "If there be any good in you, believe there is much more in others."

WEDNESDAY—MAY 26.

WILLIAM and Orville Wright, the American brothers who solved the problem of powered flight, were mechanics and self-taught inventors, yet they succeeded where trained scientists with the backing of great institutions had failed. It was not easy for them to persevere in the early days, especially when hardly anyone believed in them.

I like this story of how they received unexpected encouragement.

To obtain flying practice they needed a level field. A farmer took pity on them and let them have one free of charge. It was exactly what they needed. Even better, a Mrs Beard lived nearby. She took to watching the men with interest and concern. When the plane landed abruptly — as it often did — she would dash across the road with a bottle of her special lotion to soothe away their bruises.

I'm not saying that the Wright brothers would have failed with their experiments had it not been for Mrs Beard. I do know that somewhere in the Hall of Fame there is a little corner for her and her precious bottle of lotion.

THURSDAY—MAY 27.

ADD *a little kindness*
To your living day by day.
SUBTRACT *the kind of worry,*
That can constitute dismay.
DIVIDE *your time by turning*
Each frown into a smile.
MULTIPLY *your efforts*
For a total that's worthwhile.
J. M. Robertson.

CLIMBER'S REWARD

THE FRIENDSHIP BOOK

CAN you name the two most wonderful pieces of machinery in the world? Is your mind now rapidly running through some of the marvellous inventions of our age? Let me give you some clues — these "machines" never need oiling or greasing, never cease work until their owner lies down to rest, and even then are immediately ready for work again at the slightest cry or need. Have you guessed the answer to my question? Yes, it's a pair of human hands.

DEREK TANGYE and his wife, Jeannie, left successful jobs in London in search of their earthly paradise. They settled in a derelict cottage on the beautiful Cornish coast, built up a flower farm and lived a peaceful and simple life — helped along by the donkeys and cats that were so much a part of their family.

Tangye's books depict the essence of happiness, the absorbing simplicity of days in the country made up of small, busy things, and they reflect the values of those he meets who share the same philosophy of life.

Writing about the pedlar, known to generations of children as Uncle Albert, he says, "Money really had no value to him. He had the philosophy, the corny philosophy, of trusting people, of being kind, of being cheerful, of not being envious, of possessing the genuine wish to help without any thirst for recognition. This attitude was the currency by which he lived a happy life. I suppose he was as far as possible as free as the wind he faced every early morning as he walked the lanes of Cornwall . . ."

A splendid philosophy.

THE FRIENDSHIP BOOK

WHEN the world began, all the birds had to go to the Teacher of all Birds to learn how to look after themselves. The first lesson was about nest-making and most of the birds were there, but the jackdaw had spent all day flying around looking for treasures, and when nightfall approached she had nowhere to sleep.

"Help!" she called to the other birds. "What shall I do?" So they flew to her rescue — the sparrow, the robin, the blackbird, the swallow and the wren.

"First of all, you need a twig," said the sparrow, "and you place it on a branch like this."

"Oh, I know all about that," said the jackdaw impatiently.

"And then you find a few more twigs and balance and carefully weave them together," said the robin and the blackbird.

"Oh, I know that already," said the jackdaw.

Patiently, the swallow and the wren told her how to make the nest strong with bits of mud from the river bank, and to line it with feathers to make it soft and warm. But again, the jackdaw said, "Oh, yes, I know that."

In the end, the other birds got tired of trying to help the disagreeable bird, so they flew away leaving the jackdaw with her half-made nest. She had no idea how to finish it, and she still doesn't. To this day, her nest is just an untidy bundle of sticks — all because she was too conceited to listen to the good advice of others!

IT is God that girdeth me with strength, and maketh my way perfect.

Psalms 18:32

JUNE

I HAPPENED to be walking in the park recently, when two young ladies passed me, enjoying the sight of the beautiful flowers.

"What unusual blooms that lupin has!" I overheard one of them say.

"Yes, even the leaves are strange," agreed her friend. "But it's very pretty though, isn't it?"

They walked on, still admiring, both quite oblivious of the fact that the flower they had been praising was not a lupin at all, but a foxglove, generally considered to be a weed. Ah, well, as Shakespeare said, "A rose by any other name would smell as sweet"!

THE Lady of the House was still chuckling when she returned from a shopping expedition in town.

"Do you remember the story of the Boy Scout doing his good deed for the day who insisted on helping an old lady across the road, Francis?" she said. "Well, it happened to me today.

"I had just hesitated at the top of the escalator when a man grabbed my arm and said, 'Don't worry, dear, escalators aren't nearly as frightening as they look. Hold on to me and we'll be down in no time.'

"And so we were," smiled the Lady of the House. "I thanked him at the foot — and I hadn't the heart to tell him that I had stopped because I'd suddenly remembered something else I had to buy on that floor!"

THE FRIENDSHIP BOOK

A PRAYER

IF I stumble on the way,
Lift me up, dear Lord, I pray,
Give to me Thy helping hand,
Wisdom just to understand.

A listening ear to hear Thy voice,
A heart that makes the sad rejoice,
A tongue to speak and sing Thy praise,
And strength another soul to raise.

Arms outstretched to welcome all,
Feet to hurry at Thy call,
Eyes to see those in distress,
That I may ease their loneliness.

Give me courage to fulfil,
All I must, to do Thy will,
But if I stumble on the way,
Lift me up, dear Lord, I pray.

Dorothy M. Loughran.

NOT long ago I was fortunate enough to enjoy a most magnificent afternoon tea. We had bread and butter, strawberry jam, and a home-made fruit cake. You may be thinking that it sounds very nice, but — *magnificent*?

Well, you see, it was the first day it had been warm enough to take our tea outside in the garden. The sky was blue, the birds were singing, and the air was filled with the glorious scent of Spring flowers.

Now, tell me, in which expensive restaurant could we have enjoyed a meal that was quite so magnificent?

THE FRIENDSHIP BOOK

THE oak tree has a very special place in British history. It's one of our best-loved trees. "Hearts of oak" was a striking description of the fighting ships of old, and it's no wonder that the oak has given rise to many proverbial sayings such as "Great oaks from tiny acorns grow".

Recently I came across a less well-known saying: "Today's mighty oak is just yesterday's nut that held its ground". Surely another way of saying, "Stand fast to your faith".

AND he said unto her, Daughter, thy faith hath made thee whole; go in peace, and be whole of thy plague.

Mark 5:34

I REMEMBER reading that people often carry their talents about with them in the way that a primitive man might carry a telescope — shut up! If asked what he could see through it, he would probably say, "not very much — everything is blurred."

But if somebody took the trouble to show the man how to adjust the telescope and make use of it, what a whole new world it would open up for him!

I believe that each of us has been given a special talent that is ours alone, and nobody is too young or too old to start using it. So whether it be a newly-discovered talent, or one we have been exercising for many years, let's find time to be grateful to the parent, teacher or friend who recognised that talent — and helped us to use it.

THE FRIENDSHIP BOOK

TUESDAY—JUNE 8.

"I'VE got another riddle for you, Mr Gay!" announced my young friend, Billy, when he saw me in the garden. "Why did the farmer say 'Trespassers will be admitted free'?"

"I've no idea," I confessed.

"Because the bull will charge later," chuckled Billy.

How nice it is when youngsters consider us not too old at heart to share in their fun!

WEDNESDAY—JUNE 9.

ONE of the things that gives me great pleasure on a fine Summer's day is to be taken round a beautiful garden, whether it is one of our splendid national gardens, one of our local ones on show for the day to raise money for charity, or that of an enthusiastic friend.

I experienced an example of the last when the Lady of the House and I were invited to a coffee morning at a neighbour's house. As we strolled round the garden, she pointed out with pride her lovely blooms — gorgeous roses chosen for both colour and fragrance, proud delphiniums standing like sentinels, and a glorious array of colour in the herbaceous border.

"But," she said, "my special favourites are these silver-leaved plants, because silver has a way of bringing out the best in the other plants."

As we walked home again, the Lady of the House looked thoughtful. "I liked what Molly said about the silvery plants, Francis," she remarked. "We can't all be a prize-winning rose, but we can all be an 'encourager' that brings out the best in somebody else — and what a worthwhile role that is!"

THE FRIENDSHIP BOOK

QUARRELS are such a waste of time! Conflict and argument never do anything to improve a situation, as Brothers Brian and Kenneth realised. They were two monks who worked in the monastery garden and got on so harmoniously that they began to feel life was getting monotonous.

"Let's have an argument," said Brian. "It might liven things up a bit. I'll put this cabbage on the ground and say, 'This is my cabbage,' and then you'll say, 'No, the cabbage is mine,' and that should start a good argument."

So they began. "This cabbage is mine," said Brother Brian. "No, it's mine," said Brother Kenneth.

"Oh, very well," said Brian agreeably, "if the cabbage is yours, take it!"

FRIDAY—JUNE 11.

WITH an hour to spare one fine afternoon, I decided to take a stroll along a canal towpath. I was just in time to see holidaymakers negotiating a lock in their boat. The two young men in the party jumped ashore and wound the capstans that operated the lock gates to let the water through. Every now and then, with a great deal of effort, and much puffing and panting, they gave a mighty push to the massive wooden beams — but nothing happened.

At last, when the water level had become equal on each side, the pressure was reduced, and one quite gentle push manœuvred the gates into position. The boat was then able to pass through the lock with ease and sail off down the canal.

All of which makes me conclude that there's a lot to be said for knowing the right way to tackle a job — and then knuckling down and getting it done!

ALERT

THE FRIENDSHIP BOOK

THE Irish are a lovable people with a great sense of humour. I don't know the truth of this story which was reported in an Irish newspaper, but it deserves to be true! It said that in an Irish village one Sunday morning, three Protestant ladies visited a packed Catholic church. The priest recognised them and, wishing to show respect, whispered to his server, "Three chairs for the Protestant ladies."

The server jumped to his feet and shouted, "Three *cheers* for the Protestant ladies!" The congregation rose and responded with the heartiest of cheers.

A cheering story, indeed!

NOW the Lord of peace himself give you peace always by all means. The Lord be with you all.
Thessalonians II 3:16.

OUR friend Mary was just finishing watering her window box when I called.

"I won't be a minute," she said, as she wiped her hands, "then we'll have a nice cup of tea."

Later, as we were sitting together, she said, "I've filled the box with pansies this year, Francis. I love the colours — and if you look carefully you will see that they all have 'faces'. Some of them are smiling, some look thoughtful or shy, and a few look quite sad. When I water them each morning, their nodding heads make me feel that I have a whole company of friends just outside my window."

So now when I call on Mary, I always say hello to her friends as well.

THE FRIENDSHIP BOOK

FIVE-YEAR-OLD Jeannie and her mother had called in to see the Lady of the House, and while the grown-ups were busy discussing recipes, I took young Jeannie into the garden. Used to living in a flat, she ran round joyfully for some moments, stopping only to stare entranced at all the different colours, shapes and smells of the various flowers. Then suddenly, she gave a small shriek of alarm and rushed back towards me.

"A bee," she exclaimed tearfully. "I hate those nasty bees!"

As I cheered her up with a glass of lemonade, I discovered that the only thing Jeannie knew about bees was that they sting. She didn't yet know about honey, and how hard the bees work to produce it. As I told her, Jeannie's face brightened. "Honey tastes nice," she said. "Perhaps I do like bees after all!"

As we watched the bees busy among the lavender and lupins, I couldn't help but reflect how often we make up our minds about something before we know the whole truth.

ACHIEVING

DON'T say,
"That's too hard
To do."
Just say,
"I'll achieve."
Don't say,
"I don't understand."
Just say,
"I believe."

Anne Kreer.

THE FRIENDSHIP BOOK

THE Lady Of The House and I had called to see one of our old friends, an elderly lady with more than a year or two of retirement behind her.

As we looked out of her sitting-room window, Dorothy said, "I have had to chop down the old apple tree since your last visit. I was sad to see it go, but it was badly damaged in January's storm."

"Did you do it yourself?" said the Lady of the House. "However did you manage?"

"Well," said Dorothy, "I just tackled it a little bit at a time, so I didn't find it too difficult."

As we made our way home, the Lady of the House remarked on how sensible Dorothy was. "If only more of us tackled our problems a little bit at a time, we'd all get on a lot better."

As the saying goes, the man who moved mountains began by removing the first stone.

THE composer Eric Coates who wrote much popular music, including the theme used to introduce the radio programme "Desert Island Discs", warned in his autobiography against the danger of *always* speaking the truth.

One night while in London he was hurrying to a concert he was about to conduct, when he heard a man whistling his own popular march "Knightsbridge" and making a very poor job of it. He turned to the man and saw from his dress that he was a bishop.

"Excuse me, sir — it goes like this," he said and gave a perfectly whistled rendering of the march.

The bishop retorted, "Oh, and I suppose it was *you* who composed it!"

"Well, yes, actually it was," said Eric.

The bishop gave him a quick glance and fled.

F

THE FRIENDSHIP BOOK

THE third Sunday in June is Father's Day, defined in *Webster's Dictionary* as "for the honouring of fathers". It is not nearly so old a tradition as Mothering Sunday, for it was started in 1910 in Spokane, Washington, by Sonora Louise Smart Dodd. Some years later the custom spread to the United Kingdom.

On this day, fathers are remembered with cards and presents such as ties, handkerchiefs or socks.

I once read that the best thing a father can do for his children is to show them he loves their mother. So on their special day, let's remember all fathers, and pray for them in the responsibilities they have been given, and the homes that depend so much on their example.

AND daily in the temple, and in every house, they ceased not to teach and preach Jesus Christ.

Acts 5:42

THE Lady of the House recently drew my attention to "The ABC of My Life", written by Marlene Dietrich, star of stage and screen. In it, she listed some rules for grandmothers, including herself, and I gladly pass them on:

We must never tiptoe on other people's toes.

Be there when you're needed, but disappear when you're not.

Bear the sudden silence in your home without self-pity.

Keep both ears cocked for the call for help.

THE FRIENDSHIP BOOK

PSYCHOLOGISTS, quite rightly, are often concerned about the attitude of a child to a new baby brother or sister. They advise parents to talk about the newcomer beforehand, to keep the child informed, interested and enthusiastic about progress so that it becomes a shared experience. Then the new arrival will be happily welcomed into an understanding and fully-prepared family circle.

Here is Ebenezer Rexford's appealing account of the outcome of such a loving relationship in "Flo's Letter":

> *Dear God, the baby you brought us*
> *Is awful nice and sweet,*
> *But 'cause you forgot his toofies*
> *The poor little thing can't eat.*
> *That's why I'm writing this letter,*
> *On purpose to let you know,*
> *Please come and finish the baby.*
> *That's all, from little Flo.*

AFTER being out all day there is nothing so relaxing when I get home than removing my shoes and putting on slippers.

I looked up the word in the dictionary, and "slipper" is defined as "a loose-fitting shoe easily slipped on". I suppose that's a fair description but it doesn't really give any indication of the comfort to be gained from wearing them.

I have found that old and true friends are like a pair of slippers. They are always welcoming, comforting and reassuring. I hope that these friends feel the same way about me!

THE FRIENDSHIP BOOK

HAVE you ever owned a kaleidoscope? As a child I was fortunate enough to have one and I enjoyed many happy hours of entertainment. However hard you shook the contents of the outer case they always settled down and formed a pretty pattern. The patterns were never exactly the same — it all depended where the fragments lay.

Life is rather like a kaleidoscope. It is made up of many parts, differing from person to person, but in every case they form a pattern. Sometimes the pieces are rather drab, at other times colourful, but the components, or experiences, all make a divinely-planned pattern.

ONE year I was hoping to watch the tennis at Wimbledon on television. I switched on, and did not see the mass of faces that I had expected, but rather what seemed like a huge crowd of many-hued flowers. Yellow ones, polka dots, flamboyant florals and sugar candy shades. Then I realised it was an array of umbrellas!

As I looked at this pretty scene in the rain, I thought of Stanley Fox, the inventor of the umbrella frame. When I was once at Penistone in Yorkshire, I visited the umbrella factory nearby and saw all the work that went into the making of them.

Just think, too, of all the hard work Stanley must have put into his invention! He had been inspired by the bridge over the Menai Straits to make a grooved steel frame — strong but light.

How touched he would have been to see that cheerful "field of umbrellas" at Wimbledon and to know that his invention is still so useful! They brightened my day.

HIGH DAYS ON HOLIDAY

THE FRIENDSHIP BOOK

SOME people say that Francis Bacon wrote the plays attributed to William Shakespeare. What evidence there is for this claim I don't know, nor do I really care. That Bacon was a very wise man I do know, for he left us writings filled with wisdom and rich humanity. Take this, for instance:

"It is not what men eat, but what they digest that makes them strong; not what we gain, but what we save that makes us rich; not what we read, but what we remember that makes us learned; not what we preach, but what we practise that makes us Christians."

FROM that time Jesus began to preach, and to say, Repent: for the kingdom of heaven is at hand.

Matthew 4:17

ONLY half the year has gone by, and Anne and George are wondering what the next six months will bring.

George has been in hospital with a slight stroke, Anne had a bad fall and her right arm was in plaster, while last week, their grandson was knocked off his bike and badly bruised and concussed.

They are very supportive of each other and have many close friends. Neither complains and when asked how they cope, Anne replies that life has its peaks and troughs, and at present they are experiencing a trough. She quotes a favourite saying:

"We never ask, why me, when something pleasant happens to us, so why should we question when something unpleasant happens?"

THE FRIENDSHIP BOOK

LETTERS today are an easy and accepted part of everyday life, whether we are writing to loved ones and friends, or seeing to business matters. However, it wasn't always like this. In early Victorian times letters were an expensive luxury, far beyond the reach of the poor; postal charges were levied according to distance and anyone receiving a letter had to pay for it.

One day, Rowland Hill noticed a poor woman refusing a letter from the postman because the charge was a shilling. Concerned, he paid for the letter and gave it to her.

The woman told him that, in fact, there was nothing on the paper. It was from her son, and when he was working away from home he would send her a blank sheet at regular intervals. Being poor, she never accepted it, but its arrival told her he was alive and well.

Grieved to know that the less fortunate received no news of absent relatives, Rowland Hill used this knowledge as one of his strongest weapons in the fight for postal reform. In 1840, the pre-paid Penny Post, along with the Penny Black stamp, was introduced by the kindly, caring gentleman who had been touched by the plight of a poor woman.

KIND hearts are the garden,
Kind thoughts are the roots,
Kind words are the blossom,
Kind deeds are the fruits.
A friendly word, a kindly smile,
A helpful act, and life's worthwhile.

Barbara Jemison.

JULY

THURSDAY—JULY 1.

A FRIEND TO ALL

I DON'T make a fuss,
When I need to pray,
I don't stand on ceremony,
In any way.
I just talk to Him,
As I would to a friend,
With only one difference,
Amen at the end.
Phyllis Ellison.

FRIDAY—JULY 2.

ROSES must surely be the most popular of flowers. No other has captured the hearts of gardeners in the same way, and it is said that four out of every five gardens have roses growing in them.

The very first recorded rose garden was created in 1799 by Empress Josephine, wife of Napoleon. She sought advice from all the leading gardeners of the day, and obtained specimens of every variety of rose in the world. The garden she created at Malmaison held over 250 different kinds.

Sadly, when Josephine died, the garden fell into decline, but her dream lived on, for rose gardens had come to stay and were soon found at the grandest palaces and the humblest cottages.

Alfred Austin wrote, "I have seen one clambering rose glorify a cottage home, arrest one's step and prolong one's meditations, more than all the terraces of Chatsworth."

THE FRIENDSHIP BOOK

ONE of the most horrifying aspects of the Last War was the Japanese treatment of prisoners and natives in the Far East, including the Philippines. Soon after hostilities had ceased, a Mrs Llano from the Philippines and a Mrs Eumura from Japan met at a Christian conference.

The atmosphere was naturally strained, and at first Mrs Llano could think only of the wicked acts of the Japanese towards her family.

Later that evening, there was a knock at her door. It was Mrs Eumura and she asked if Mrs Llano could possible forgive her people for what they had done?

As they clung to each other and then knelt together in prayer, Mrs Llano found to her surprise that she could forgive after all — her animosity had vanished.

The story reminded me of what the hymn writer and poet George Herbert once said: "He who cannot forgive others breaks the bridge over which he himself must pass".

BUT now, O Lord, thou art our father; we are the clay, and thou our potter; and we all are the work of thy hand.

Isaiah 64:8

CHILDREN have a logic all of their own!
It was a very hot day and we had taken our neighbour's granddaughter, little Katie, for a walk. The sun seemed to get hotter by the minute, and we were all beginning to flag when young Katie piped up, "I wish I had my cardigan on."

"Whatever for?" we chorused.

"Well, then I could take it off!" she replied seriously.

G

THE FRIENDSHIP BOOK

WHEN I was young, a boy called Geoffrey lived nearby. We used to go to Cubs and Scouts together and in Summer we often shared picnics in the country. Gradually, however, we went our separate ways. Geoffrey now owns several companies and as chairman, is a wealthy man.

To my surprise our paths crossed again recently, and he asked me if I would join him on a visit to old haunts. So now, a little more slowly than all those years ago, we tramped along the same paths reminiscing about our boyhood — his business life completely forgotten.

He told me that it was when he was on holiday in the Cotswolds — the first proper break he'd taken for years — that he found real gold, "sungold" as he calls it. He had parked his car and walked in the twilight by the river. The sky, the corn, the river — everything was golden-hued. It was breathtaking.

"At that moment," Geoffrey told me, "I knew what true gold really is, I couldn't put it in my pocket, or put it in the bank — but it is now stored in my heart. We cannot get along without all our material possessions, Francis, but it is important to keep their importance in perspective."

Such wise words!

HAVE you heard the story about the minister who was puzzled because he couldn't identify the letters H.W.P. inscribed on a stone slab in his church? He spent considerable time searching through the parish registers to match the initials with a name, but to no avail. Eventually, the mystery was solved — the letters stood for "Hot Water Pipe"!

H

THE FRIENDSHIP BOOK

THE Lady of the House and I enjoy doing the crossword puzzle in our daily newspaper. Sometimes we manage to complete it easily, other times we are still struggling with some of the clues at bedtime! Often we are just about to give up altogether when the penny drops with a certain clue. As the Lady of the House says, "It's amazing the difference one more letter can make."

It's so true in life, too. Often when things seem too difficult to cope with, another person's kindness or our own resolve to look at the problem from a different angle can make all the difference and give us the determination to succeed.

PETER is the dedicated gardener in our local park. It is always immaculate, a pleasure to sit in on sunny days, Summer or Winter.

One morning, I saw him engrossed in a letter as he stood beside his wheelbarrow. "Look at this," he said with a smile.

I read the short note. It was addressed to the park keeper, and said:

"I have spent a lot of time in your park this Summer since having a massive heart attack in February. I'm much better now, and back at work, and I would just like to say thank you for keeping the park so nice."

"I've been working here for seven years," Peter said, "but this is the first time anyone's ever said thank you to me."

It's easy to take for granted what is around us every day. The words "thank you" are simple, but are sadly under used. Yet they can mean so much.

THE FRIENDSHIP BOOK

SEA SUNDAY is one of our more recent days of remembrance. Each year on the second Sunday in July we think about those whose livelihood takes them to sea — sailors, deep sea fishermen and lifeboat men. Their work is often dangerous, keeping them from families for long periods, and Sea Sunday gives us the opportunity to remember them with gratitude.

One of the organisations set up to help is Mission to Seamen which has centres in ports all over the world. All races and creeds are welcomed by them and given support and counselling — or simply the chance to have a rest, a cup of tea and a chat. On the wall of many of their chapels is this Seaman's Psalm:

"The Lord is my Pilot, I shall not drift. He lighteth me across the dark waters; He steereth me in the deep channels. He keepeth my log. He guideth me by the star of holiness for His name's sake. Yea, though I sail through the tempests and thunders of life, I shall dread no danger, for Thou art with me. Thou preparest a harbour before me in the homeland of eternity. Thou anointest the waves with oil, my ship rideth calmly. Surely, sunlight and starlight shall follow me all the days of my voyaging, and I shall rest in the port of the Lord forever."

THE Lord shall reign for ever and ever.

Exodus 15:18

DON'T look for the faults as you go through life;
But if perhaps you find them,
'Tis wiser and kinder to turn a blind eye,
And seek for the virtues behind 'em!

TUESDAY—JULY 13.

WILLIAM JAMES COLE had lived for most of his long life in Belfast. He loved Cavehill with its great cavern where he played as a boy and the scene over the Lough as the ships sailed in and out with the tides.

Latterly he lived alone, but he still had his friends and he found solace in his hobby of painting. Then, he grew frailer, and he moved to an old folk's home in England to be near his family. For several months he was extremely lonely and unhappy until, one day, with trembling hands he looked out his painting materials and from memory painted scenes from his boyhood in Ireland. A journalist from a local newspaper happened to visit the home with the intention of writing an article. He met William James, saw his work and asked if he would illustrate the article.

From then on, life started all over again. At 87, William James Cole found himself drawing cartoons regularly for the local newspaper.

It's never too late . . .

WEDNESDAY—JULY 14.

A SUNDAY School teacher had been telling the story of the Prodigal Son to her class. She carefully explained the younger son's sorrow and repentance after his wrongdoing, and his return home. She also explained the father's joy at welcoming back his lost son and his preparation of a celebration meal.

"But there was someone for whom that feast brought only bitterness and resentment," said the teacher. "Do you know who it was?"

"Yes, miss," said one eager little boy. "It was the fatted calf!"

FAMILY GATHERINGS

THE FRIENDSHIP BOOK

THE Lady of the House was in a philosophical mood.

"There's no clash of colours in Nature's paintbox," she remarked, looking round the garden with satisfaction. "Look, Francis, there's white, the colour of peace and purity; and here is a delicate pink, the colour of gentleness; over there is blue and softest lavender, the colour of serenity; here is pale primrose and golden yellow, the colour of sunshine; and over there is tawny bright orange, the colour of vitality, and scarlet, crimson and glowing coral, the colour of fire. There's a flower for every one of my moods — and all to be found within my own back garden!"

It reminded me of some words written by William Cobbett:

"Some persons may think that flowers are of no use, that they are nonsensical things . . . I hesitate not a moment to prefer the plant of a fine carnation to a gold watch set with diamonds."

OPTIMISM versus pessimism is a much discussed topic, but I enjoyed reading Joyce Hifler's definition and think it is worth passing on:

"An optimist questions life the same as a pessimist, but the difference is he knows that there is an answer and he knows that he will find it. He is aware that the cherries which life is supposed to be a bowl of, have stones, but he is prepared to remove them. His mind does not dwell on the hardness of the stones, but on the sweetness of the cherries."

What a positive and helpful attitude that is! As the old saying reminds us: "brooding over our troubles is the surest way to hatch more."

THE FRIENDSHIP BOOK

THERE is a considerable difference of opinion about the correct way to address church dignitaries.

I like the story told of the late Archbishop William Temple before his move from York to Canterbury. A shy young aspirant for Holy Orders called at Bishopthorpe, palace of the Archbishop of York, and knocked on the door which was opened by none other than the great man himself.

Nervously, the young man explained that he did not quite know how to address an Archbishop. "Well," said Archbishop Temple, "my friends call me Bill."

AND Jesus, when he came out, saw much people, and was moved with compassion toward them, because they were as sheep not having a shepherd: and he began to teach them many things.

Mark 6:34

THE art teacher began her classes with her students one day by setting up something for them to draw, an awkward plant with several trailing stems. It looked very difficult until she pointed out a mark of reference — a poster on the wall behind the plant.

"If you refer to that, it will help you to get the perspective right," she said.

The class took her advice and found the drawing much easier to do. It is always worth remembering that if we are able to focus on the good and true values in life, we will always get our perspective right.

TUESDAY—JULY 20.

LITTLE songs to make me glad,
Little comforts when I'm sad,
Little chores at last well done,
Little laughs and bits of fun,
Little ills which happen not,
Little nods that mean a lot,
Little children to caress,
Little deeds of tenderness;
Such a wealth of little things
To my spirit richness brings.

Barbara Jemison.

WEDNESDAY—JULY 21.

ONCE we went on an excursion along the South Tyndale Railway's short length of track, the highest narrow-gauge railway in England. The three carriages and a guard's van were pulled by the engine "Thomas Edmondson" — named after the inventor of the traditional card railway ticket.

Our carriage was full of enthusiastic people, all interested in different things — steam trains, travel, bird watching, and hillwalking. We were soon all chatting as if we were old friends.

As the steam from the engine billowed skywards, and its whistle echoed around the fells, we saw the Tyne sparkling in the sunshine, drystone walls and shady woodland, and a curlew rising from the fields. On the return journey, the scent of wild flowers drifted through the windows.

Back at Alston, we all enjoyed homemade cakes at the station café while the "Thomas Edmondson" had his water replenished.

What made that day so special was that we shared it with others and enjoyed their company. Isn't this true of so many good things in life?

THE FRIENDSHIP BOOK

IN an Italian village it was the custom to carry a large statue of the Madonna in procession through the streets. The statue was very old and made of brown clay, which had become grimy with age. The face was not at all beautiful and it was known as "The Ugly Madonna".

When a new priest came to the village, he suggested that, rather than be carried by four men, the unwieldy statue could, with dignity, be carried on an open lorry. The priest secretly hated the statue and hoped that it might fall and break as the lorry made its way along the bumpy cobbled streets. Then, as it rounded a steep incline the statue fell and shattered.

The villagers gasped — at first with horror and then with delight. For inside the clay was revealed another statue — a beautiful carved one. It had been hidden beneath the clay for safety many years before in time of war. Now it was carried back to the church with pride and became known as "The Fair Madonna".

There is often beauty beneath an ugly exterior. It is wise not to judge anything or anyone by outward appearance alone.

THERE is a nice little story told of Wolfgang Amadeus Mozart, the musical genius who started playing the piano when he was only three.

One day, his father asked him what he was doing, and he replied, "Looking for little notes which like each other." As good a definition of musical harmony as you could find.

It seems to me that this idea could be extended to world harmony. It just needs a lot of little people to find out that they could like and respect each other, and world-wide peace would then be possible.

SATURDAY—JULY 24.

DOROTHY, a neighbour of ours, has a penfriend who lives at the other end of the country, and they have corresponded for nearly 40 years. During that time letters have flowed to and fro regularly, sharing plans for weddings, telling of additions to the family, children's progress, and later, news about grandchildren. However, during all these years Dorothy and her friend have never met, and I asked her recently why this was so.

Dorothy smiled. "We did once think of arranging a meeting," she admitted, "but at the last minute we both decided against it. You see, we feel we already know each other as well as we ever can, and so often outward appearances serve only to get in the way."

Wise words indeed.

SUNDAY—JULY 25.

FOR there is one God, and one mediator between God and men, the man Christ Jesus.

Timothy I 2:5

MONDAY—JULY 26.

THE Lady of the House is not very fond of spiders. If she catches sight of one I am quickly summoned to remove it. I find many people share her dislike of the web-spinners.

However, none of God's creations is useless, and spider-haters might find a lesson in these words of Leo Tolstoy:

"The means to gain happiness is to throw out from oneself like a spider in all directions, an adhesive web of love, and to catch in it all that comes".

A charming thought, and a lovely way of looking at spiders and their webs.

TUESDAY—JULY 27.

MY dictionary tells me that a house is a dwelling, but when I looked up "home", I found that there was a subtle difference. It was defined as "the place where one lives", "a family living in a house" or "something viewed as a place dear to one". Here are some apt quotations on the subject.

"This was one of my prayers: for a parcel of land not so very large, which should have a garden and a spring of ever-flowing water near the house, and a bit of woodland as well as these."   (Horace, 65-8 B.C.)

Mid pleasures and palaces though we may roam,
Be it ever so humble, there's no place like home.
(J. H. Payne)

"But all that I could think of, in the darkness and the cold, was that I was leaving home and my folks were growing old."   (R. L. Stevenson)

"A house with daffodils in it is a house lit up."
(A. A. Milne)

To my mind, Edward Whiting expresses it best of all:

"You can no more measure a home by inches or weigh it by ounces, than you can set up the boundaries of a Summer breeze, or calculate the fragrance of a rose. Home is the love which is in it."

WEDNESDAY—JULY 28.

LORD SOPER, the great Methodist preacher, was once visiting a church in Chicago. After the service they proudly showed him a crèche which had been set up for young children and babies whilst their parents were at their devotions. Over the door was a printed notice bearing a text from St Paul which read:

"We shall not all sleep, but we shall all be changed"!

EXPLORERS

THURSDAY—JULY 29.

I HAVE just paid a visit to our local rubbish dump. What useful places they are! It's always good to see people taking the trouble to use them.

It was very satisfying to part with our rubbish — an old chair, odds and ends from the garage, and a pile of old timber that I had kept for years in case it ever came in useful — which it never did! I came home pleased with my morning's work and glad that there was now more space in the house for things that really mattered.

It made me think about other things we hold on to unnecessarily — suspicions, grudges and uncharitable thoughts. How much better to get rid of them all and make room for the important things in life!

FRIDAY—JULY 30.

HAVE you heard the story about the two ladies who were discussing the sermons delivered the previous Sunday?

"Well, I liked the minister's best," said the first lady. "He said 'Finally' and finished, but the curate said 'Lastly' and lasted . . ."

SATURDAY—JULY 31.

HARRY was an old tramp who begged his way from town to town, and seemed quite content with his lot.

One day, he was given an old jacket. Later, in an inside pocket he found a pound coin. He returned to the house and said that he'd found it.

"You're an honest man," said the householder.

"Thank you, sir," said the tramp, "is there any chance of getting the waistcoat and trousers as well?"

AUGUST

AND, Thou, Lord, in the beginning hast laid the foundation of the earth; and the heavens are the works of thine hands.

Hebrews 1:10

STINGING nettles,
Thorny hedge,
Holly, with its
Prickly edge;
Honeysuckle,
Brambly rose,
This is how
My garden grows!

Elizabeth Gozney.

I AM sure the Lady of the House and I are not alone in admitting that when we are on a long journey, we are so keen to arrive at our chosen destination that we pay too little attention to the places we pass through on the way.

Several years ago, we travelled to the north of Scotland, passing through what were, to us, just place-names on the way. We realised afterwards that we should have taken time to look at the towns and villages en route.

The whole of our lives can be likened to making a journey. If we are always looking too far ahead — to the next outing, the next holiday, the next day even, we miss the pleasure that each day brings. Better to enjoy life as it is now, today, this very moment.

THE FRIENDSHIP BOOK

THE daisy tends to be a rather unappreciated little flower, simply because it is so common. Our lawn is full of daisies. On a sunny day they are scattered across the grass like summer snowflakes. I hate to cut off their heads when I mow the grass, though I need not really worry, for they always come up again, prettier than ever.

They are like the ordinary folk we all know and take for granted — young mothers bringing up children, or older women looking after elderly relatives, the assistant in the shop, the woman in the queue, the driver of the bus. They all have their ups and downs, their setbacks and disappointments, but they keep bouncing back, holding their heads high again — just like the daisies.

IT is a great mistake to regard ministers as perpetually serious, with no time for fun and laughter. On the contrary, most ministers of religion I have met have had a good sense of humour and appreciated the amusing side of life, especially the strange things that are bound to happen in the course of their work.

Phil Mason of Kettering made a collection of church anecdotes which were published under the title "Christian Crackers". Here is an example:

A vicar was talking to the parents of a baby they had brought for baptism. He found to his surprise that they were to name the boy after himself.

"Why are you going to do that?" he asked. "Are you hoping to make a parson of him?"

"Oh, no!" the father said. "He'll have to work for his living!"

FRIDAY—AUGUST 6.

"JUST listen to that, Francis," said our friend Mary as we sat in her small back garden that day enjoying the last rays of Summer evening sun. She pointed to her chimney pot where we could see a blackbird singing his heart out in a rich, sweet succession of musical notes.

"I'm certain it's the one that my Tibby attacked last week," she said. "I was so upset, but I managed to rescue it and shut Puss in the kitchen until the bird was able to fly away. Now I've noticed that it comes to sing on the roof every evening. I hope you don't think I'm being fanciful, Francis, but I'm certain he comes back just to say 'thank you' to me."

True or not, that bird gives Mary a great deal of pleasure. The world would be a sad place indeed without birdsong.

SATURDAY—AUGUST 7.

OUR friend Eric had been staying with us for a short holiday, and soon after he had gone home we received a thank-you letter from him. He, too, must prefer letters to phone calls — anyway, it made us feel very pleased and very "special".

The letter had a different sort of ending. Eric didn't say "yours sincerely" or "from your old friend" or even with "all good wishes". He wrote:

The Love of Christ surround you,
The Light of Christ lead you,
The Peace of Christ fill you,
The Power of Christ assist you,
The Joy of Christ thrill you,
The Presence of Christ be with you always.

I hope that you will find this blessing as helpful and comforting as we did.

H

SUNDAY—AUGUST 8.

AND to you who are troubled rest with us, when the Lord Jesus shall be revealed from heaven with his mighty angels.

Thessalonians 1:7

MONDAY—AUGUST 9.

MRS BROWN is an elderly lady we have both known for many years. As the Lady of the House and I passed one day, she was about to walk down to the shops. Her son Robert, now in his forties, was seeing her off at the door.

"Now take care, Mother," he called out as she stepped over the threshold, "and look properly when you cross that busy road!"

"He's always like that," said Mrs Brown once the door had closed and we were standing at the gate. "It's nice, I suppose, but I sometimes wonder, who does he think taught *him* to cross the road?"

With that she set off briskly down the street.

TUESDAY—AUGUST 10.

THERE is a board hanging in our kitchen. On it we write down items needed for shopping, plus messages and reminders. It is made of plastic and we use a thick red pencil on it. Recently there wasn't any space left to write on. However, it was a simple job to clean it — a quick wipe over with a soapy cloth and the slate was clean.

We can wipe the slate clean in our lives, too. Perhaps there is an apology to be made, a promise to keep, a thank-you that has been left unsaid. Don't leave it any longer — wipe the slate clean and start again.

THE FRIENDSHIP BOOK

JANET was telling me how difficult she and her family had found it to settle when they moved house. One of the children was unhappy at school, and she and her husband seriously considered going back to their old home, which was still unsold.

"Then," said Janet, "I met a cheerful old gentleman who stopped and said, 'Hello, I don't know your face. Are you new here? Isn't it a lovely day?'

"That meeting," she said, "changed our whole outlook. The old gentleman became very dear to us all and introduced us to a host of new friends. We've never regretted moving — in fact, we bless the day we did!"

I WILL never forget a memorable Summer's evening when the Lady of the House and I were in the Lake District. It was beautiful when we left for our walk, but, as dusk descended, so did the mist. We lost all sense of direction. Suddenly, the pathway branched into two.

"Which way do we go now?" asked the Lady of the House anxiously.

We peered into the darkness and caught sight of a tiny glow. It came from a shepherd's cottage we had passed on the way.

"If we keep our eye on the light," I said, "we can't go wrong." So we watched the light, sometimes faint, sometimes clear, sometimes nearly disappearing, but by keeping our eye on that lamp, we came safely through the darkness.

There is always a way out of every difficulty and perplexity — His light is always there, showing us the path to take.

THE FRIENDSHIP BOOK

HERE'S a message of encouragement sent in to me by Barbara Jemison:

> *You're lucky if you do not strike*
> *Before so very long*
> *A day when every blessed thing*
> *Seems somehow to go wrong.*
> *But don't despair, don't tell yourself*
> *That you are finished quite,*
> *Keep plodding on, and grin until*
> *Most everything is right.*

SLEEP was proving difficult one night not long ago. I tried counting sheep, but it didn't help. I then reviewed the events of the day. I thought first of the things that hadn't gone right — the sort of minor irritations that happen to us all.

To begin with, I had overslept and started the morning on the wrong foot. Then, driving into town, I had been stuck in a traffic jam. Later in the day, a friend I was hoping to meet was unable to turn up and finally, on reaching home, I found that I had forgotten to post an urgent letter.

The pleasant parts of the day were seeing our garden in full bloom on a sunny day, and receiving good news from a relative overseas. Then there was an act of unexpected thoughtfulness from a neighbour and an appreciative word of thanks for a little job I'd done.

All things considered, when I thought about it, the good parts of the day cancelled out the bad ones. It put things into perspective and, as I thought about all this, I fell asleep. Perhaps you'll find that this approach may help when you're next having difficulty nodding off.

THE FRIENDSHIP BOOK

JESUS said unto him, If thou canst believe, all things are possible to him that believeth.

Mark 9:23

THE rose with its amazing variety of colours and perfumes is usually regarded as perfection amongst flowers.

One of the loveliest stories connected with it is about the queen who lay dying. A wise man said that if she set eyes on the purest and most perfect rose on earth, she would live. The queen was greatly loved and all the people brought their most beautiful roses to her bedside, but to no avail.

At last her small son came into the room carrying a book with gold clasps. When the queen opened it, she saw a picture of Mary nursing the Holy Child. From that moment she made a rapid recovery to good health. She had seen the most beautiful rose on earth.

THERE'S a world of difference between a mischievous child and a really naughty one. We may frown at the latter, but often find ourselves smiling at the harmless mischief-maker. I enjoyed a story I read about the boy whose antics made his mother exclaim, "How do you expect to get into heaven?"

He looked thoughtful for a moment and then replied, "I shall just run in and out and keep slamming the door until they say, 'For goodness sake, either come in or stay out' — and then I'll go in!"

I'm sure even St Peter would have to smile at that!

THE FRIENDSHIP BOOK

I MET one of my neighbours in the park the other day. I stopped for a chat and also to stroke her little dog, Kelly. She hasn't had Kelly very long, for she had another dog, Cindy, who died.

"When I lost Cindy after 17 years," Joan told me, "I was broken-hearted. The vet tried to persuade me to get a new dog, but I said I would never, ever have another because I couldn't bear the pain of parting again. Then," she said, "my birthday came along, I was alone in the house and feeling very down. I said to myself, here you are with lots of love and plenty of time to spare, and the RSPCA must have dogs that are needing a good home. So I went to their kennels, and there was Kelly, thin, nervous, her coat in a terrible condition — and my heart went out to her."

"I can find you a much better dog than that," said the RSPCA official, but my neighbour had already accepted the challenge of looking after Kelly. She took her home, bathed her, fed her and stayed up most of the night with her.

"She has cost me pounds in vet's fees," Joan laughed, "but look at her now! She's a lovely little companion and worth every penny I spent."

Anyone who loves animals will know exactly what she meant.

MONEY will buy a bed, but not sleep; books, but not brains; food, but not appetite; finery, but not beauty; a house, but not a home; medicine, but not health; luxuries, but not culture; amusements, but not happiness.

Which all reminds us, once again, that the best things in life are still free.

THE FRIENDSHIP BOOK

NOT FOR SALE

I DON'T think you'd want it,
  It's quite rough to feel,
It's a tattered old thing,
  With little appeal.
It's too shabby to use,
  Being faded and old,
But you couldn't have this,
  If you offered us gold.
It's Grandmother's quilt,
  Her patchwork creation,
A token of love,
  For each generation.

Phyllis Ellison.

OUR friend Dora has proved — with astonishing persistence and courage — the wisdom of the saying, "If at first you don't succeed, try, try, try again."

She was in her late fifties when her husband died. She had never learned to drive, but decided she must do so at once. She took lessons, and eventually passed the driving test — but not before failing 18 times!

Each time she tried it she would get into such a state of agitation that she made foolish mistakes. What torture she endured! Many people would have given up trying, but persistent, courageous Dora overcame her nervousness at last and finally got through.

Have you noticed that any lasting success has, more often than not, been achieved against a background of failures, setbacks and disappointments? It is how we meet these obstacles that determines our destiny.

SEA, SAND AND SUN

THE FRIENDSHIP BOOK

AND Jesus went forth, and saw a great multitude, and was moved with compassion toward them, and he healed their sick.

Matthew 14:14

ARE you a stargazer? I enjoy looking skywards, although I don't possess a telescope. I'm quite happy on a Summer's evening to sit in the quiet of our garden and look up at the stars.

August and December are the months when you can see shooting stars, and not long ago I watched a spectacular one fall to earth. Of course, it isn't practical to sit outdoors in December, but on a clear night, warmly wrapped up, I will venture out for a brisk walk to look up at the sky. At this time of year, I am always reminded of the Three Wise Men who saw a new star foretelling the birth of the Saviour.

It is the same sky that they gazed at, and we can all feel part of the continuity of our wonderful world.

A LOT of fishing stories are concerned with the big ones that got away. This little yarn takes a very different look at the subject. You can believe it if you like!

A man stopped his car to watch a fisherman on the river bank. First the angler hooked a large pike — and threw it back. Then he caught a beautiful trout — and threw that back, too. Then he landed a tiny perch, grunted with satisfaction, and put it in his bag.

The observer called out, "Why on earth did you throw the two big ones back and keep the tiny one?"

Came the reply, "I've a small frying-pan!"

THE FRIENDSHIP BOOK

I HAVE been enjoying reading "A Country Calendar" by Flora Thompson, best known for her delightful country classic "Lark Rise to Candleford". Written in the 1920s, it is a series of sensitively drawn little pieces from the observations of a down-to-earth countrywoman.

In the following cameo, she describes her meeting with the village shepherd whose philosophy of life she is so in tune with:

"A penny for your thoughts, Shepherd!" I called across the road to him.

For answer he pointed to the full moon riding in a fleece of pearly clouds above the line of the down. "They can't put that out," he said, "nor the sun, nor the stars, for all their mightiness. To see her shine like that makes you feel that it's only just on the surface that things 'as come to such a pass and at bottom all is as the Lord intended; and everything will be as it has been again, even though we mid not live to see it."

As the old shepherd moved away with quiet dignity, the writer confessed: "My own heart had been full of bitterness, and I felt rebuked, although comforted. As I walked on I marvelled that such a man should have been born to a life of obscure toil."

It is good for all of us to meet someone who can help us to see things in the right perspective.

I T had been rather a long service in church, or so little Katie thought, and she was beginning to grow restless.

Suddenly, in a quiet spell between hymns, her clear little voice piped up, "Mummy, is it *still* Sunday?"

THE FRIENDSHIP BOOK

I RECENTLY came across these lines attributed to Francis Bacon, the poet and philosopher. They were written a long time ago, but are as true today as they were then:

"There is nothing purer than honesty; nothing sweeter than charity; nothing warmer than love; nothing richer than wisdom; nothing brighter than virtue; nothing more steadfast than faith".

GROWING old is not something we look forward to, but it does help if we can retain a sense of humour. I am told that these verses, sent to me by a Yorkshire reader, were written by an 80-year-old man from Bradford to cheer up a friend in hospital:

When people's cars get old and worn
And they begin to toddle,
They go somewhere and trade them in
And get the latest model.

Now I have very often thought
That when my joints get achey,
And when my hair has all turned grey
And knees are very shaky,

And when the onward march of time
Has left me rather feeble,
How nice t'would be to find a firm
That deals in worn-out people.

And when my form is bent with age
And gets to looking shoddy,
How nice it would be to turn it in
And get a brand new body!

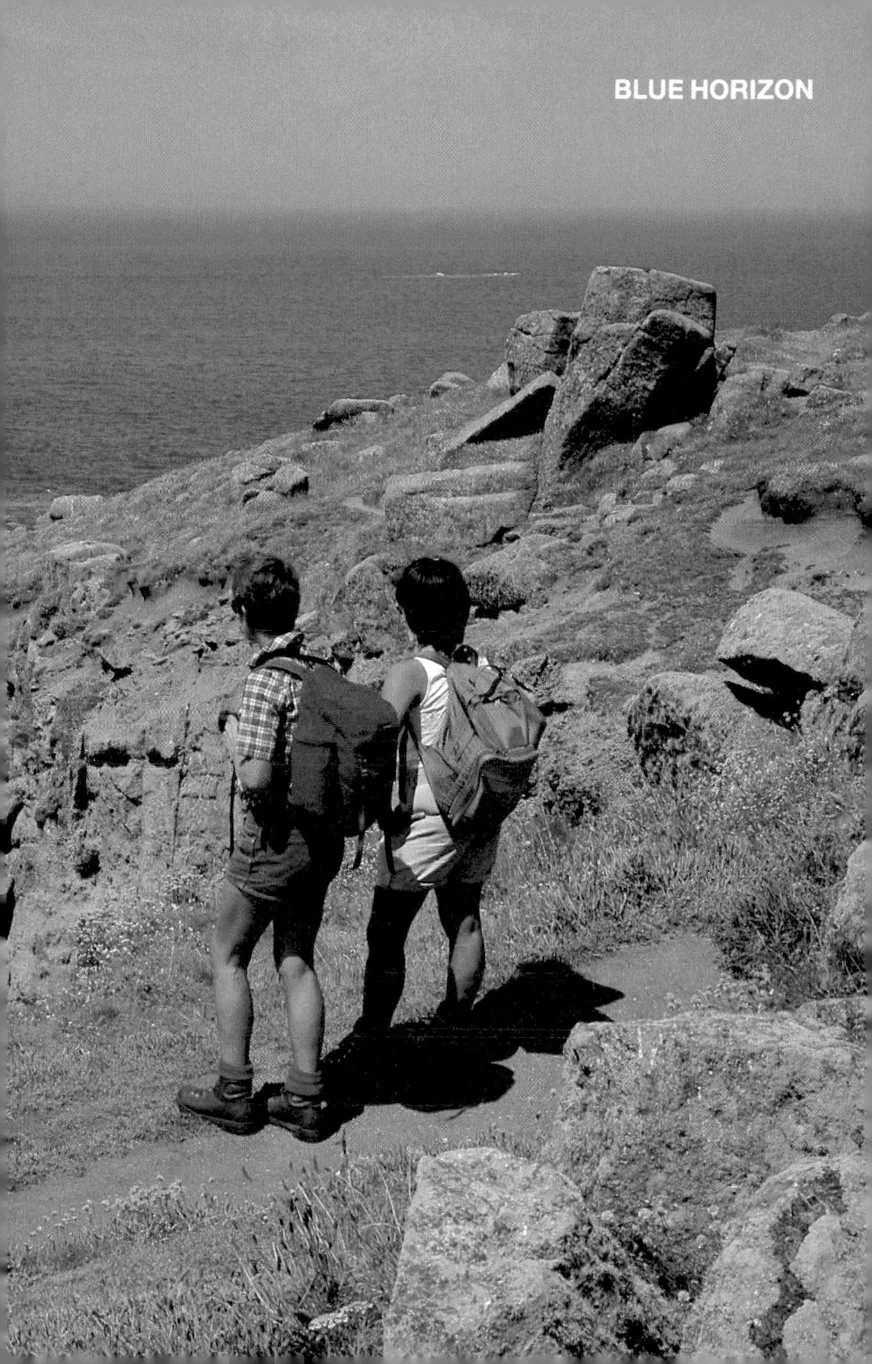
BLUE HORIZON

SUNDAY—AUGUST 29.

CAN any hide himself in secret places that I shall not see him? saith the Lord. Do not I fill heaven and earth? saith the Lord.

Jeremiah 23:24

MONDAY—AUGUST 30.

WHAT a special relationship there can be between a small child and his grandparents! I am thinking of little Thomas who had been looking forward to a visit from his grandparents. They all had a most enjoyable time.

When they had to set off home again, Grandma went upstairs to say goodbye to Thomas. The bedroom looked as if a tornado had hit it.

"What are you doing, Thomas?" asked Grandma.

"I'm sorting out some toys to take with me when I go home with you tonight," replied the youngster.

"Does Grandad know you're coming?" said Grandma.

"No . . ."

"Does Mummy know?"

"No . . ."

"Well, let's go and ask her," suggested Grandma.

And of course, his mother agreed. In no time at all, a little suitcase had been packed and two delighted grandparents drove home with a precious little bundle in the back of their car.

TUESDAY—AUGUST 31.

I ONCE heard that fine singer and good Christian, Sir Harry Secombe, say this:

"Always judge a person by the way they treat someone who can be of no possible use to them."

Thank you, Sir Harry!

SEPTEMBER

WEDNESDAY—SEPTEMBER 1.

CAROLE M. PICKWORTH of Rustington, West Sussex, came across this old poem and sent it to me. I'm glad she did, because it expresses a lovely thought:

Life is sweet just because of our friends,
*   And the things which in common we share;*
We want to live on, not because of ourselves,
*   But because of the people who care.*

It's giving and doing for somebody else,
*   On that all life's splendour depends,*
And all of the joys of this wonderful world
*   Are found in the keeping of friends.*

THURSDAY—SEPTEMBER 2.

WE pruned our rose hedge last year, cutting out all the dead stems. As a result, we enjoyed a magnificent display of roses during the Summer.

People passing stopped, smelled their perfume and admired their beauty — they were a joy to behold. Now, as Autumn approaches, the bushes are covered with fat rosehips, fine fare for a pair of greenfinches. Rosehips have a beauty of their own, especially after overnight frost.

You don't have to be in the youthful bloom of life to be admired — mature years bring with them a different beauty and a wealth of experiences to share:

As a white candle in a holy place
So is the beauty of an aged face.

COUNTRY DELIGHT

FRIDAY—SEPTEMBER 3.

HOW easy it is to become impatient and frustrated when things don't seem to be progressing quickly enough for us.

I have been reading about Carla Maria Giulini who is recognised as one of the world's leading conductors. He is now in his seventies, but he waited more than 20 years before he performed the music of the great composers Bach, Beethoven and Mozart — just because he did not feel ready to tackle them.

He said, "I have to understand a score, believe in it and love its every note. If those three conditions have not been fulfilled, then I cannot conduct the work."

Truly, the best things are always well worth waiting for!

SATURDAY—SEPTEMBER 4.

WE went to see our friend Mary recently, and found that a bad bout of bronchitis had laid her low. However, she was just as cheerful as ever and eager to pass on little pieces of news from other visitors.

"I don't know how you manage to keep so cheerful, Mary," I said. "What is your secret?"

"Well, Francis," said Mary serenely, "I have such a lot to be thankful for. I may not be a star at present, but there's no reason at all why I should be a cloud."

It's not surprising that Mary's visitors come away feeling better for having spent time with her.

SUNDAY—SEPTEMBER 5.

THE earth is the Lord's, and the fulness thereof; the world, and they that dwell therein.

Psalms 24:1

K

THE FRIENDSHIP BOOK

HAVE you sometimes found that it can be difficult to stick to your principles? You've been tempted to take the easy way out of a dilemma? Just remember the wise man who said:

"Streams become crooked from taking the path of least resistance — so do people."

GOD comfort you at close of day,
And when small stars begin to peep,
Re-make you in His own dear way,
By giving deep, refreshing sleep.

God comfort you, when falls the night,
When there is stillness everywhere,
And from the roses, red and white,
A fragrance issues as of prayer.

God comfort you for all the strain —
The cares and stresses of the day,
Make you in spirit whole again,
And wipe each falling tear away.

God comfort you, as falls the dusk,
O'er roof and cottage, vale and tree,
The birds find shelter, where they must,
And earth is wrapped in mystery.

Could there be sweeter time than this?
The turning of the light to dark,
When something of High Heaven's bliss,
Is given to every human heart?
                    Margaret M. Dixon.

THE FRIENDSHIP BOOK

I DON'T remember the author of this very old verse, but isn't it a positive message for us today — and every day?

If I can live a life that tells on other lives,
And make the world less full of anguish and of pain;
A life, that like the pebbles dropped upon the sea,
Sends its wide circles to a hundred shores;
May such a life be mine.

WITH the holiday mood upon me, I have been dipping again into those delightful books by Derek Tangye, "The Minack Chronicles". In them, with charm and humour he describes how he and his wife Jeannie decided to escape from the rat race of London and settle in an isolated cottage on a Cornish flower farm. Here they acquired a family of loved animals — the cats Lama, Monty, Ambrose and Oliver, and the donkeys Penny and Fred, and later, Merlin. With these companions and in these tranquil surroundings, the Tangyes discovered a completely different way of life, and were enchanted by it.

Describing the relationship he enjoys with his pets, Tangye writes: "Animals offer stability in this unstable world. They do not deceive. They soothe jittery moods. They offer solace in times of trouble by the way they listen to you. They may not understand a word you say, but that doesn't matter because it is a dumb sympathy that you ask of them and they give it; an extra-sensory understanding, which is the more comforting since it is secret. You have no regrets afterwards for having disclosed too much."

Any animal lover will know exactly what he means!

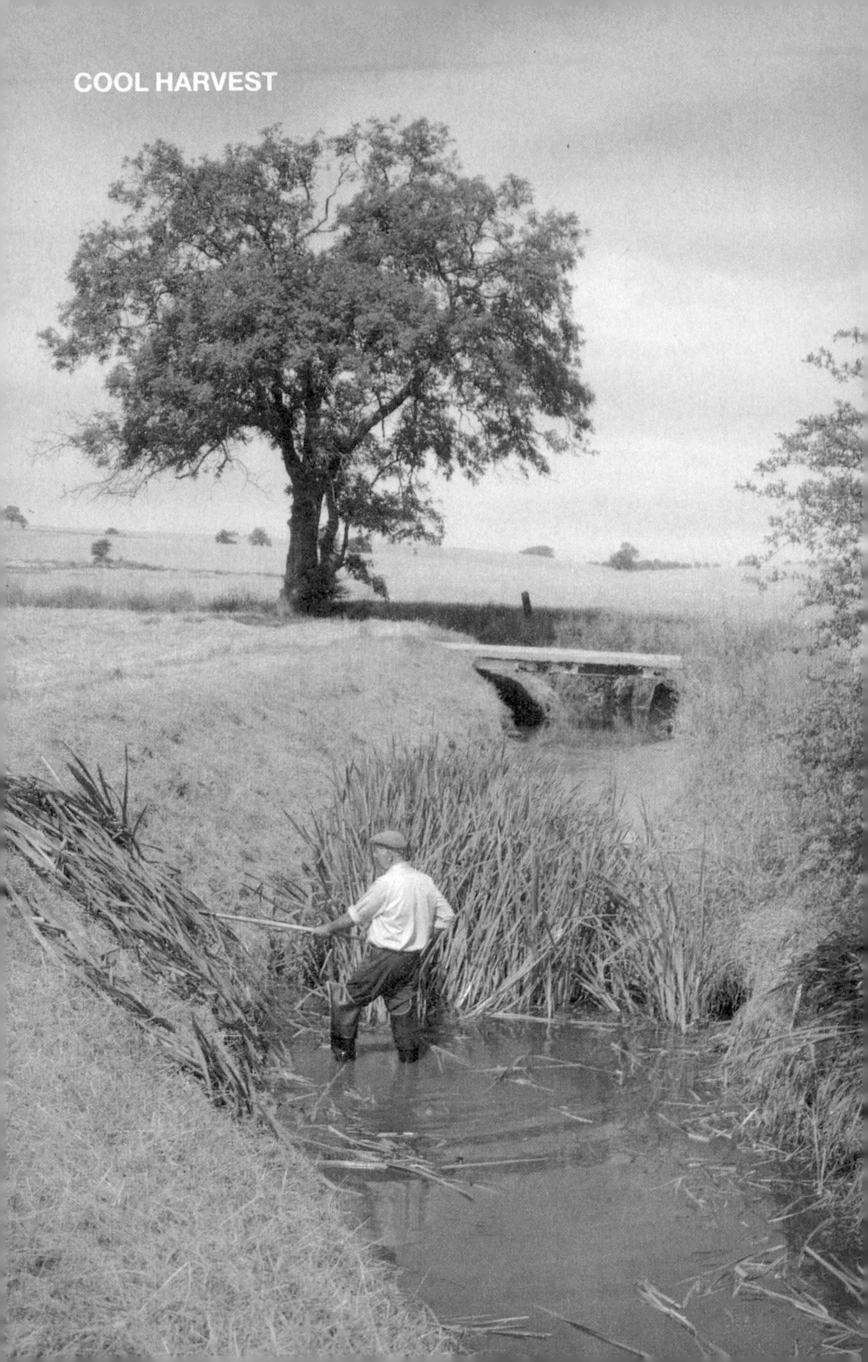
COOL HARVEST

THE FRIENDSHIP BOOK

A FRIEND told me of an enterprising clergyman who delivered a letter with these printed instructions to each of his parishioners:

"Please hold this page close to you, blow on it, and look carefully at the result. If the paper turns green, call your doctor, if brown, then call the dentist, if red, call your bank manager, if black, then call the undertaker. Should this page remain the same colour as it is now, you are in good health and quite able to come to church next Sunday. I look forward to seeing you!"

I don't know how many turned up that Sunday, but I'm sure the message wasn't wasted — a little humour can work miracles.

ALEXANDER THE GREAT once decided to give a lot of things away. To one man he gave a small fortune, to another a whole province, and to yet another a very lucrative string of bazaars.

"If you keep on doing that," remarked one of his friends, "you will have nothing left."

"Don't you believe it!" retorted Alexander. "I have kept for myself the most valuable thing of all."

"What is that?" asked his friend.

Alexander smiled. "My hopes for the future," he replied.

THE night is far spent, the day is at hand: let us therefore cast off the works of darkness, and let us put on the armour of light.

Romans 13:12

THE FRIENDSHIP BOOK

"*THERE is a time,*" *said God,*
    "*For understanding.*
"*There is a time,*" *said He,*
    For knowing all the reasons.
"*And everything shall happen*
    In its time," *said God,*
"*Each thing to its time*
    And all men to their seasons."

Jean Harris.

ALONG with many other people, one of the highlights of the year for the Lady of the House and me is the Last Night of the Proms from the Albert Hall in London. We take care to be comfortably settled in front of the television in good time, so that we don't miss a minute of it.

It is a uniquely British occasion, noted for its exuberant audience participation. A cynic said that the audience makes up in enthusiasm what it lacks in musical skill, but, in fact, the majority of the young Promenaders are serious music lovers and may have spent night after night listening to music during the season of Promenade Concerts.

I heard that in 1989 the Promenaders collected £3,500, from which they bought the traditional garland for the bust of the founder Sir Henry Wood, buttonholes for the orchestra and a bouquet for the soloist. The remainder was donated to musical charities, including the recently launched Jacqueline du Pré Fund.

I salute those young music lovers, not only for their enjoyment which is so infectious — but for their generosity in helping others.

THE FRIENDSHIP BOOK

IN the garden of a primary school, the children, with the help of their teacher, planted an unusual apple tree. It is known to gardeners as a "Family Tree" on which three types of apple can grow together and it was developed by horticulturalists to give variety in small gardens.

This tree seemed to reflect the values and aims of the school, which nurtures children from different homes and of different races, creeds and colours.

The pupils waited excitedly to see if the tree would indeed produce different kinds of apples. In time, they noticed the tiny fruit developing and to their great delight, they later grew into the three promised varieties — all on one tree!

One afternoon, the children gathered round the tree and each picked an apple. As they munched the crisp fruit, their teachers told them, "If clever people can make trees like this and we can live in friendship and harmony in our little school, then there must always be hope for peace in our world."

WHEN I think of Barnsley in Yorkshire I think, not of a colliery town, but of the grit and tenacity of people who have survived disasters and unemployment, yet are still smiling, still proud of their town and surrounding countryside.

Three miles away stands Wentworth Castle, now a college, and in the grounds is one of Britain's greatest rhododendron gardens. For some years they fell into neglect, but they have been rescued and lovingly restored.

Come what may, endurance and fortitude — in man and Nature — will never be suppressed. They will always blossom forth.

FRIDAY—SEPTEMBER 17.

I VISITED a craft fair recently, and among the exhibitors were a husband and wife, both handspinning. The Lady of the House and I watched as a crowd gathered round to listen as they explained their craft in detail. In the crowd was a small group of blind people and I wondered what they were gaining from being there.

I moved closer and listened to the exchange of questions and answers as the blind people touched first the fleece and parts of the wheel, then finally the spun yarn. It was wonderful to see the lively interest on their faces as they grasped what was happening. Sadly, many other exhibits must have been lost on them, as not everyone took time to explain what they were doing.

We are all guilty at times of assuming that when one sense is absent, then the remaining senses must be absent, too! This isn't so, of course. Those blind people touched the wheels and wool with sensitive fingers and keen intellects, as though the loss of their sight had heightened their other senses.

I am sure that He who created us is responsible for restoring the balance.

SATURDAY—SEPTEMBER 18.

PUBLILIUS SYRUS was a Roman philosopher who lived away back in 42 B.C., yet how up-to-date are many of the thoughts he left us!

Take these, for instance:

"No man is happy who does not think himself so".

"Prosperity makes friends, adversity tries them".

"It is better to have a little than nothing".

"An agreeable companion on a journey is as good as a carriage".

CAREFREE

THE FRIENDSHIP BOOK

SUNDAY—SEPTEMBER 19.

AFTER this manner therefore pray ye: Our Father which art in heaven, Hallowed be thy name.

Matthew 6:9

MONDAY—SEPTEMBER 20.

SIX-YEAR-OLD Peter was taken to his first Harvest Festival. Among the offerings of fruit and flowers, the bunches of purple grapes on the pulpit took his fancy. When the offertory box came round, he put in a twenty pence piece and said confidently, "Grapes, please!"

TUESDAY—SEPTEMBER 21.

CATHERINE N. REES of Derby came across this poem by an unknown author. It offers good advice for every traveller on life's highway:

Don't find fault with the man who limps
Or struggles along the road,
Unless you have the shoes he wears,
Or stumble beneath his load.

Don't be harsh on the man that sins,
Or pelt him with words or stones,
Unless you are sure, yea, doubly sure,
That you have no sins of your own.

Don't sneer at the man who's down today,
Unless you have felt the blow
That caused his fall, or felt the pain
That only the fallen know.

You may be strong, but still the blows
That were his, if dealt to you,
In the self-same way, at the same time,
Might cause you to stagger, too.

THE FRIENDSHIP BOOK

RABBI LIONEL BLUE once told this story:
"My dog was quite happy with one toy — a plastic chop that squeaked when she chewed it. But trouble came when an admirer gave her a companion toy, a plastic bone that squeaked. Though she was a big dog, she had only one mouth, and her jaw could not accommodate both the squeaking bone and the squeaking chop. She picked up one, then noticed she was without the other. So she dropped the former and picked up the latter and had the same situation in reverse. Laboriously, she tried it again with the same result. Bemused, she looked at bone and chop, and then throwing back her head she howled at the tragedy of it all. Her affluence had not brought her contentment."

It's something that many of us have already discovered — that the richest person may be the poorest of all when it comes to the things of real and lasting value. No matter how much wealth the richest person may appear to have, they cannot have everything that this world has to offer. The key to real success and contentment lies in richness of the spirit, a wealth of untold importance which each and every one of us can possess if we so choose.

A. J. CRONIN, famous for his novels such as "The Citadel" and "Hatter's Castle", was well-known also as a writer of inspiring articles.

He had the ability to put profound wisdom into a few brief words. Many people, for instance, must have been helped by his saying, "Worry never robs tomorrow of its sorrow; it only saps today of its strength."

THE FRIENDSHIP BOOK

MANY years ago, an old violin had come up for sale in a miscellaneous collection of items at an auction. It was so scratched, battered and dusty that the auctioneer thought it hardly worth bothering with. However, he held it up and began the bidding. "Who will give me a shilling?" he asked. "Two? Who'll make it three? Going for three shillings."

Then, from the back of the room came an old man. He picked up the violin carefully, wiped the dust from it, adjusted the strings, and taking the bow he began to play. The melody he played was pure, sweet and breathtaking.

In the quiet room the auctioneer started the bidding again. "What am I bid for the old violin? Who will give me a thousand pounds? Two? Who will make it three? Going for three thousand pounds . . . Gone!"

Everyone clapped, but one man said, "I don't understand. What changed its value?" The reply came, "It was the touch of the master's hand."

As I say, it is an old story, but there are many today who can testify to the change in the worth of their life through the touch of the Master's hand.

TO all dear friends I'd like to say
That life's all rush and hurry.
I've scores and scores of daily chores
Besides a lot of worry.
But it is true (you'll know it, too)
There's two sides to a penny,
Though much is wrong, I sing a song
Because my joys are many.

Barbara Jemison.

THE FRIENDSHIP BOOK

THEREFORE I will look unto the Lord; I will wait for the God of my salvation: my God will hear me.

Micah 7:7

OFTEN, when I offer a chair to a visitor, I am reminded of an old saying quoted by a friend on a day when I was indulging in a mild grumble:

"You can't stop trouble from coming to you, but there's no need to give it a chair to sit on!"

THE work of Mother Teresa in Calcutta is well known. She left her convent, trained as a nurse, and then worked in the slums, taking in abandoned babies, lepers, giving refuge to the dying, the lonely and the hungry.

In 1979 she was honoured by being awarded the Nobel Peace Prize, yet she remained the modest and caring person that made her one of the most loved people in the world. I know she never regarded herself as a philosopher, but just listen to some of the things she has said:

"Money is very necessary, but we must take care to increase its value by seasoning it with love."

"For leprosy I have a cure, for tuberculosis I have a cure. But for being unwanted and unloved there is no cure, unless there are willing hands to serve and a loving heart to love."

"Spread love everywhere you go: first of all in your own home."

"Let us always meet each other with a smile, for a smile is the beginning of love."

THE FRIENDSHIP BOOK

A SURPRISE telephone call has given me a great deal of pleasure. It was from a friend many miles away who phoned to say that she had been reading the thought for the day in her "Friendship Book".

"I had to speak to you, Francis," she said. "Sometimes your pieces make me laugh, sometimes I shed a little tear, but today I felt it had been written especially for me. It was just what I needed. It cheered me up and set me right for the whole day."

It's nice when we have something good that we can share with others. What can *you* share today?

HERE are some jottings from my notebook on the subject of prayer:

Now that daylight fills the sky,
I lift my heart to God on high.
(5th century Christian hymn)

Lord through this hour be Thou my guide,
That by Thy power no foot shall slide.
(Prayer for the quarters of the hour)

"The Christian on his knees sees more than the philosopher on tiptoe." (Dwight L. Moody)

"Any concern too small to be made into a prayer, is too small to be made into a burden."
(Corrie ten Boom)

And, finally, there is the sticker which my friend has on the window of his car:
Life is fragile — treat it with prayer!

OCTOBER

FRIDAY—OCTOBER 1.

L AST Autumn in broad daylight I watched a squirrel gathering nuts from our hazel tree to hoard away for the cold days of Winter.

Are you a hoarder? I confess that I am. I hoard birthday cards, books, letters, newspapers, photographs . . . The list is endless as the Lady of the House would readily agree!

I also hoard memories of happy occasions when all our family are together. These stand me in good stead when the miles separate us all. Then I hoard in my mind's eye a beautiful sunset or sunrise for when the days are dark and grey in January. I also like to store away in my head a stirring piece of music which will return to cheer me when I am feeling downhearted.

Of course, some kinds of hoarding are wrong, but the kind of hoarding I'm talking about never did anybody any harm and does the hoarder a whole power of good!

SATURDAY—OCTOBER 2.

F RIENDSHIP is always invaluable, particularly when, as in the case of Mrs D. Hayes of Avon, you are disabled and unable to get out and about much. On her Golden Wedding Anniversary, Mrs Hayes' daughters arranged a celebration with 92 guests — a token of the family's love and devotion.

Mrs Hayes sent me this verse:

Isn't it lucky that you and I
Have something that money cannot buy,
A joy that is real and has no end —
The joy of having and being a friend.

THE FRIENDSHIP BOOK

SUNDAY—OCTOBER 3.

AND Jesus returned in the power of the Spirit into Galilee: and there went out a fame of him through all the region round about.   Luke 4:14

MONDAY—OCTOBER 4.

I WONDER how many readers have heard of Dr Herman Boerhaave?

In the 17th century he was one of Holland's most successful — and expensive — physicians. When he died, a curious provision was found in his will. He said he had written a book revealing the deepest secrets of the Art of Medicine, and he ordered that it be put up for auction.

Bidding was keen and the book cost the successful buyer a huge sum of money. He seized his purchase, hoping to find within, the secrets of a long and healthy life, but opened it to find 99 blank pages. There was nothing until page 100 where it said, "Keep your head cool, your feet warm, and you will make the best doctors poor."

We don't know if he thought the advice dear at the price, but if he followed it and enjoyed good health, it was probably the bargain of the year.

TUESDAY—OCTOBER 5.

I OVERHEARD a conversation recently between a father and his two sons who had been for a walk in the woods and had found some chestnuts still in their husks. The children were amazed that such a prickly outside could contain something so sweet within. Their pockets were full of the lovely glossy nuts.

Some people are like chestnuts. If we take the trouble to penetrate the outer layers of their reserve, we may find a heart of sweetness and kindness under the prickly exterior.

K

THE FRIENDSHIP BOOK

SOME time ago I was reading L. P. Hartley's book "The Go-Between," and I was struck by a remark in it: "The past is a foreign country — they do things differently there." Well, is that true?

Things always were a bit different in the past, especially the way of life, but have you noticed how older friends demonstrate to us time and again by the lives they live how they have learned a lot by experience? Wrongs have been righted, mistakes have been noted, and not repeated. Surely this is how life is meant to be lived.

The past, with its mixture of good and bad times, forms the foundations of the present and, in turn, those of the future.

CATCH the moment as it happens,
Catch the moment as it flies,
All the world is full of magic,
If we only use our eyes.
See the sky on starlit evenings,
Touch the petals of a rose,
Hear the pop of roasting chestnuts,
Marching bands at village shows.
Cobwebs on a foggy morning,
Washing on a windy day,
Sunshine on a polished table,
All are magic in their way.
Take the time to stop and wonder,
Catch the moment, lest it dies,
Such enchantments may be fleeting,
Brief as Autumn butterflies.

Margaret Ingall.

THE FRIENDSHIP BOOK

I DON'T know much about the teachings of the ancient Greek philosophers — Aristotle, for example — but it is some comfort to know that I am not alone in this. We ordinary mortals find we can get along quite nicely without burdening our brains with abstract ideas. I was encouraged, too, to read that Aristotle's ideas were not always correct, as a modern philosopher, Bertrand Russell, showed when he wrote:

"Aristotle could have avoided the mistake of thinking that women have fewer teeth than men, by the simple device of asking Mrs Aristotle to keep her mouth open while he counted. He did not do so because he thought he knew. Thinking that you know when, in fact, you don't is a fatal mistake."

Or as my old teacher once said, "Do you know what thought did? He didn't, he only thought he did!"

THE Lady of the House had been feeling a little down. There had been a chapter of accidents early that morning. First of all, the washing line had broken, dropping all the clean clothes on the ground, then she locked herself out and next, a pan of milk boiled over. Not a good start to the weekend!

Then, through the letter-box came the first of the new season's bulb catalogues with lovely colour pictures of golden daffodils, crimson tulips, delicate snowdrops and bright crocuses. As we looked through it and made plans for the garden, we both soon forgot the irritations of the morning.

It can take only a very small thing to lift somebody out of despondency. Just as a small incident can cast you down so another, apparently quite trivial, can raise your spirits sky-high.

THE FRIENDSHIP BOOK

MY tabernacle also shall be with them: yea, I will be their God, and they shall be my people.

Ezekiel 37:27

I CANNOT help wondering what Irving Berlin might have achieved had he had the benefit of a formal musical education. He was born in Russia, but was taken by his parents to live in America when he was a child, and his first attempt at earning his living in the world of music was as a singing waiter.

Berlin never learned to read music, yet his inexhaustible inventiveness produced successful songs for more than half a century. He wrote everything in the key of F sharp, and a lever under his specially-constructed piano transposed his music into other keys.

Amongst his thousand or so toe-tapping songs are many that will not quickly be forgotten — "Putting On My Top Hat", "Easter Parade", "There's No Business Like Show Business", "I'm Dreaming Of A White Christmas" and the music for "Annie Get Your Gun".

So, if we are ever tempted to think we could have done a lot better if only life had given us more opportunities, it's worth remembering the example of Irving Berlin!

IN the course of a sermon, our minister quoted these lines and I'm sure you'll agree that they make a worthy thought for the day:

Love is a basket with five loaves and two fishes;
It's never enough until you start to give it away.

READY!

THE FRIENDSHIP BOOK

FRANCES REED lives in Oban, amidst spectacular Highland scenery. She expresses her thanks for the wonders of Nature around her in these lovely words:

For all the glory of the way,
For friends to share it each new day,
For sea and sky,
And loch and hill —
Oh, Lord my God,
I thank Thee still.

For lonely glen and heather track,
For tide-washed sand and brown sea wrack,
For heron's flight
And peewit's call,
For thundering roar
Of waterfall,

For windswept moorland's Autumn hue
And snow-capped hills in distant view,
For rowan-tree
With berries red,
Most loving Lord,
My thanks are said.

IT'S surprising how much can be said in a few words, which is why I like reading the mini-sermons on church noticeboards.

Two of my favourites are these:

"Don't pray that your load may be lightened, but that your back may be strengthened to bear it!"

"Where the faithless may see only a hopeless end, the faithful rejoice in endless hope."

FRIDAY—OCTOBER 15.

IN the Autumn of 1989 I went to Southwark in South London to see the archaeological remains of Shakespeare's Globe Theatre, and then went to see his church — now called Southwark Cathedral. Here he would often worship and visit his brother's grave. I saw his memorial and thought how hard he worked in his short life to give enjoyment to others.

I found another memorial, too, set in the floor. Around it were words from the Song of Solomon: "Many waters cannot quench love." It reminds us that in 1989, 51 young people died when their boat sank in the Thames, near to this waterfront church. Someone had placed on it a small bunch of flowers.

I walked out into the twilight thinking of these young people and those who had tried to save them. I had gone inside the church to remember a famous man, but came away remembering ordinary people and the sincerity of that little floral tribute and its message.

SATURDAY—OCTOBER 16.

WHEN I think of Abraham Lincoln, I think of a great President of the United States, a lawyer who espoused good causes, and an opponent of evils such as slavery. When I read this anecdote recently, I also found that he had a dry wit which, on occasion, he would use to rebuke those who were too full of themselves.

Lincoln was taken by a friend to see an acclaimed canvas by an indifferent artist. He looked at the picture and commented, "The painter is very good and observes the Lord's Commandments. I think that he hath not made to himself a likeness of anything that is in the heavens above, or that is in the earth beneath, or that is in the waters under the earth!"

THE FRIENDSHIP BOOK

HOW great are his signs! and how mighty are his wonders! his kingdom is an everlasting kingdom and his dominion is from generation to generation.

Daniel 4:3

FEELING depressed about the coming of colder weather? Don't! I'll tell you why:

Gone are the long, bright Summer days,
Now Autumn fires are aglow.
Soon the trees will shed their leaves
And colder winds will blow.
But what care I what ills and chills
The coming days may bring?
There never was a Winter yet
Which did not turn to Spring!

MANY years ago, I had to make a difficult decision, one that required a lot of heart-searching. I visited an old and valued friend to seek his advice. "I'd go ahead," I explained to him, "if only I was sure I would succeed."

He listened, and then said, quietly, "Be bold. Mighty forces will come to your aid."

I took his advice, and have been grateful to him ever since.

The dictionary definition of bold is, "Courageous, enterprising and confident."

There are hidden capabilities in all of us — skills, creative ideas, energy and a strength and endurance far greater than we imagine; they are there for us to discover — and use.

THE FRIENDSHIP BOOK

OUR corner shop has been taken over by a new couple, Phil and Margaret. They are pleasant, hard-working young people so I hope they will make a success of their venture. On the counter they have one of those motto cards that are so popular nowadays. It says:

"If you see a customer without a smile — give him one of yours!"

When I remarked on it, Margaret said, "Well, Mr Gay, not all customers are as easy to deal with as you are, and it serves as a reminder to me that people may come into the shop feeling ill, unhappy or out of humour, but however difficult it may be, it is my task to serve them as best I can."

I was put in mind of some words that William Barclay wrote as a prayer for shop assistants:

"Help me to be patient with the time-wasting, courteous with the discourteous, forbearing to the unreasonable. Make me such that people will go away happier, and smiling because I served them today."

It's a prayer we could use whenever we are going to be in contact with other people.

HAVE you ever wondered why some people live to such a grand old age?

On the occasion of her 100th birthday, Catherine Bramwell-Booth, the granddaughter of Salvation Army founder William Booth, had this to say:

"I'm in love with life, and life is loving. If you haven't learned to love someone else better than yourself, you haven't begun to live."

There's a message there for all of us, young and old.

THE FRIENDSHIP BOOK

I LIKE this verse entitled "The Master Weaver". It's a reminder that even in the things that perplex us, our lives are safe in the hands of Him who made us:

The pattern of our lives is formed with tender loving care,

And He who does the weaving works in colours dark and fair.

We see odd strands of colour as the tapestry unfolds,

Not understanding there must be greys among the golds.

But in the Master Weaver's eye the whole design is clear,

For He alone knows why and where the dark threads must appear.

And if we trust His guiding hand, then one day we shall see

The final picture woven in a perfect tapestry.

A PRIZE was once offered to the artist who could paint the best picture depicting peace. Some painted beautiful landscapes, quiet villages, sleeping children, or a quiet country home. But the winner of the prize painted a violent storm — the roaring sea, dashing waves, black clouds and treacherous winds. When you studied the picture you saw, high on a cliff, a little bird in a small crevice, sitting securely in perfect peace.

The artist was showing the world what faith is all about. No matter how insignificant we seem to be, we can always find a place of peace amidst the storms of life.

THE FRIENDSHIP BOOK

SUNDAY—OCTOBER 24.

AS long as I am in the world, I am the light of the world.

John 9:5

MONDAY—OCTOBER 25.

WHEN I was browsing around our local bookshop, I found a volume explaining how to use time efficiently, to help make life happier and more productive for ourselves and for others. This made me think of something I had recently read about Dame Cicely Saunders, the founder of the Hospice Movement.

She said something about time that I had not thought of before. As a doctor, she had been lecturing at one of the London hospitals about the hospice movement and explaining how the work is organised at her own St Christopher's Hospice in London.

"It's all very well, but you have time to spare," said a pompous consultant who had 90 beds, and registrars and housemen to help him.

Dame Cicely, who was responsible for 120 beds, replied crisply, "Oh, no, Doctor, time isn't a question of length, it's a question of depth, isn't it?"

We must always make time for kindness, thoughtfulness and sympathy.

TUESDAY—OCTOBER 26.

I LIKE the story of the small girl saying her prayers who was heard to whisper, "God bless Daddy and Mummy, and brother Jack. God bless me — and, dear God, do take good care of yourself for if anything should happen to you what would become of the rest of us?"

THE FRIENDSHIP BOOK

I CAME across a definition the other day which is new to me: "A bore is a person who talks about his rheumatism when you want to talk about yours!"

I think a lot of us need now and again that shrewd little reminder that one of the secrets of happiness is to be more outward-looking, and to overcome our own aches and pains by paying attention to someone else's. Remember the words of the Bible: "The Lord turned the captivity of Job when he prayed for his friends."

LOST a loved one? Feeling lonely? These comforting verses "To A Widow" by Iris Hesselden may help to ease the ache in your heart:

Come, dry your tears, smile again, love,
I'm only a whisper away,
Near in the dusk of the evening,
Just out of sight through the day;

Watching you waking and sleeping,
Hearing each prayer that you pray,
Sending my love to surround you,
I'm only a whisper away.

Come, dry your tears, smile again, love,
Remember the good times we've known,
Cherish the joy we discovered —
Love that was planted and grown.

Your road may seem lonely ahead, love,
And distant horizons look grey,
You won't be walking alone, dear,
I'm only a whisper away.

THE FRIENDSHIP BOOK

IT'S October! The clocks have been put back and the evenings are gradually drawing in, the lawn has had its final trim and garden tools have been cleaned and put away until the Spring. Any outdoor activities after supper are abandoned now in favour of indoor pursuits. But I have no regrets. I can cheerfully echo the words of William Cowper in 1783:

"I see the Winter approaching without much concern, though a passionate lover of fine weather and the pleasant scenes of Summer. But the long evenings have their comforts, too; and there is hardly to be found upon earth, I suppose, so snug a creature as an Englishman by his fireside, in the Winter."

What a blessing that the seasons come round as they do to give us rest and variety just when we need them!

WE aren't born naturally skilful. We may be born with a talent, but whether or not it develops is entirely up to us.

"How did you learn to skate?" I once asked a competitor after she'd won a competition.

"By getting up every time I fell down," was the reply.

And if we do just that, there's no telling what we can achieve at the end of the day.

AND now abideth faith, hope, charity, these three; but the greatest of these is charity.

Corinthians I 13:13

NOVEMBER

MONDAY—NOVEMBER 1.

WE were standing outside the house one Winter's evening seeing off friends who live in the heart of an industrial city.

They both looked up at the starry sky and remarked how much more noticeable the stars were here than they ever see them at home. There the bright lights, smoke haze and tall buildings tend to obscure them.

In the same way, up on high moors or beside the sea, the sky often seems wider and clearer than usual.

The same is true of life. When problems and petty affairs crowd in, our appreciation of the joy of living is squeezed out. It's only when we step back and create space around us that the wonder and beauty of it all once again floods over us.

TUESDAY—NOVEMBER 2.

OUR friend Phyllis has "green fingers" and says that her idea of Heaven is of one enormous and beautiful garden. I once talked to a minister who said he couldn't imagine what Heaven would be like, but he had a graphic picture of "The other place".

"I can imagine it would be like being trapped in a huge, overcrowded supermarket at peak times with no way out through the check-outs!" he declared.

Wherever our imagination may lead us, the relationship of Heaven to Earth is well expressed in a thought I read in a church magazine: "We are not citizens of this world trying to make our way to Heaven; we are citizens of Heaven trying to make our way through the world."

THE FRIENDSHIP BOOK

A FRIEND has been telling me that he has joined a creative writing class. He is not expecting to write a best seller, but enjoys making up short stories and poems and sharing his efforts with others.

One day, the class was encouraged to write a poem about the one thing which really made their lives worth living. Several sincere, serious and wordy poems were produced. However, the one poem which the tutor liked best was this, written by an elderly gentleman:

Fairest to me of all delights
   That makes this earth a heaven,
Is the joy of finding it's half-past six,
   When I thought it was half-past seven!

How nice to take pleasure in small things, and with a sense of humour!

WHEN I was a boy and came home with my clothes covered in mud, as small boys often do, my mother used to say, "We'll leave it for now. It will brush off when it has had a chance to dry." Sure enough, after a few hours the mud brushed off, leaving hardly a trace.

I often think about this when angry words are exchanged. It's the easiest thing in the world to want to retaliate if we are offended or our feelings are badly hurt, but usually it only makes matters worse. It's far better to let things rest until we feel calmer, so avoiding a quarrel that might be difficult to heal.

The old saying reminds us that "least said, soonest mended", whilst the writer of Proverbs in the Bible wisely advises us that "a hot-tempered man stirs up dissension, but a patient man calms a quarrel".

THE FRIENDSHIP BOOK

I MUST admit to being a bit of a stickler about not wasting electricity, so when I noticed that our hall light had been left on, I quickly switched it off.

"Please don't, Francis," said the Lady of the House. "I left it on deliberately. Old Mrs Brown across the road happened to mention that she always looks across on a dark Winter evening, wondering if we are at home. If she sees a light in our house, it makes her feel so much more at ease and comfortable. So now I'm going to leave a light on, whenever we're at home, just to let her know we're here."

After I'd heard this, having that extra light burning didn't bother me one bit!

I AM always amused when I recall the story of a chorus girl who was offered the present of a book by an admirer. She replied, "No, thanks, I've already got one!"

The philosopher Erasmus once said, "When I get a little money I buy books; if any is left I buy food and clothes."

Two extreme views for us to think about today! What is certain is that with the possession of even a few favourite books, we are never without friends, and they are always there to turn to for comfort, advice or entertainment.

A ND now come I to thee; and these things I speak in the world, that they might have my joy fulfilled in themselves.

John 17:13

HISTORIC WATERS L

THE FRIENDSHIP BOOK

<u>MONDAY—NOVEMBER 8.</u>

A FRIEND was 40 recently and I sent him a card of congratulations. He is a very active and able person and I knew he was more than a little regretful at leaving the thirties behind, so in the card I wrote the following words by Benjamin Franklin to settle his fears:

> *At twenty years of age, the will reigns;*
> *At thirty, the wit;*
> *and at forty, the judgment.*
> I hope he felt his wisdom growing!

<u>TUESDAY—NOVEMBER 9.</u>

WITH a few minutes to spare on a cold November morning, I stood by our sitting-room window and watched the last tawny-coloured leaves of our cherry tree flutter to the ground. The frost of the past day or two had severed the remaining life in them and now it needed only a gentle breeze to leave the tree quite bare. It was hard to imagine that only six months before, the same tree had been covered in a fairy-like cloud of pink blossom.

Until I saw the tree stripped of its leaves, I don't think I had appreciated all of its beauty, the straightness of its trunk, the lovely markings on the bark and the graceful branches silhouetted against the Winter sky.

So often the same applies to our relationships with people. It is easy to pick up a wrong impression about somebody and allow it to become permanent. However, if we take the time and trouble to get alongside them, with all superficial things stripped away, we may find quite a different person underneath — and sometimes with a beauty we have never suspected.

M

THE FRIENDSHIP BOOK

MORNING THOUGHTS

SEEK a fresh goal every day,
  Look on all things new;
Show a smile along the way,
  Let happiness shine through.
Don't give up when your plans fail,
  Make another start;
Keep a trust if hope is frail,
  And faith within the heart.
Set aside a time to care,
  And then you'll find it's true:
A kindness passed around to share
  Will be returned to you!
                    Elizabeth Gozney.

CHARLES HITT, a watermelon farmer in America, kept bees, because they like melons. He had an affinity with the insects, and they sensed his affection. He worked and handled them without trouble and he was never stung.

Charles died on a bleak Winter's day when there was not a bee to be seen. However, at the funeral a great buzzing was suddenly heard during the graveside service, and a cloud of bees appeared and flew around in a strange manner. It was as if they knew that their friend was dead. They came in masses, covering every lovely blossom on the grave. Later, Charles's son found that the bees had left the hives — never to return.

The story shows the extraordinary bond that can exist between humans and bees. If it can be so strong, how much more powerful is friendship between people.

THE FRIENDSHIP BOOK

AN elderly friend called Violet, is a great animal-lover. She has a cat of her own and also feeds three others which come to her door. One of them is very timid. It jumps down from the flat roof of the garage next door to feed and then disappears back up there.

One day, we were visiting Violet and watched as she spoke to the cat on the roof. To my surprise Violet took a thick garden cane, reached up, and tickled the cat round its ears. It responded by rolling about and rubbing its head round the cane.

"This cat is too nervous to be stroked on the ground so I have to show it love by remote control," she said.

When we reached home, I thought about the wisdom in her words. They sum up our relationship with God. Whilst we are here on earth we cannot touch Him, but His love for us is there if we stretch out towards him.

I HAD a chuckle at this story I was told recently.
A spell of severe weather and an outbreak of flu had sadly depleted the congregation and, as the minister surveyed the tiny choir and sparsely-filled pews, he announced with great feeling, "Our first hymn this evening is 'Oh, for a thousand tongues to sing . . .' "

AND Jesus said unto them, Come ye after me, and I will make you to become fishers of men.

Mark 1:17

THE FRIENDSHIP BOOK

YOU may grow older in years, but your spirit can remain sensitive, receptive and alert — your actual age ceases to matter. Maybe you're doubtful about this. Well, think about these people: Edison was still experimenting at 83; Goethe, the German dramatist, wrote "Faust" at 82; Benjamin Franklin helped shape the American Constitution at 81; Cato, who lived in the days of the Roman Empire when Greek culture was invading Rome, set himself to learn Greek at 80; while Titian painted his noblest masterpieces at 98!

Encouraging, isn't it?

LITTLE LAMPS

AS little sparks within the dark,
　　Are chosen words a friend may say,
Like tiny lights within the night,
　　They guide us on our pilgrim way.

A little laugh — a little fun —
　　A little sweet hilarity,
These lamps are lighted, one by one,
　　To bring new hope to you and me.

A little warmth — a little love —
　　Some help received — a good deed done,
And heartache tends to disappear,
　　As mists before the rising sun.

Seldom by acts of courage made,
　　Is our spirit made to shine,
But we are led 'neath threat'ning shade,
　　By little lamps along the line.
　　　　　　　　　　Margaret M. Dixon.

THE FRIENDSHIP BOOK

WE enjoyed a visit to the local playgroup on their open day recently. It was good to see the little ones playing together happily and constructively, supervised by a team of volunteer mothers. Near the door a large poster caught my eye: "Have you hugged your kid today?" It was intended for the parents who used the playgroup, yet it was a reminder that *all* of us need to demonstrate our love to those nearest and dearest to us.

Someone once said: "A good hug is a perfect gift. One size fits everybody and nobody minds if you exchange it."

However, I can't help having sympathy for the young lad in a story told by Robert Runcie, former Archbishop of Canterbury. He saw a book in a shop window with the title "How To Hug". It was at a bargain price, so he rushed in, paid his money — and discovered he had bought an odd volume of an encyclopaedia!

IT is essential to hold on to our ideals, to look up and not down, for nothing is ever achieved in life by constant pessimism. Once, when he was Prime Minister, Ramsay MacDonald was discussing with a government official the possibility of lasting peace. The official, an expert on foreign affairs, was unimpressed by the Prime Minister's idealistic viewpoint. "The desire for peace does not necessarily ensure it," he remarked cynically.

"Quite true," admitted Ramsay MacDonald. "Neither does the desire for food satisfy your hunger, but at least it gets you started towards a restaurant."

A wise remark which gives us food for thought today!

FRIDAY—NOVEMBER 19.

"HER name was Joanna. She came into the ward each morning like a little song bird, happy and smiling."

So said a good friend of ours who had just spent some time in a busy hospital. He was referring to a junior nurse whose mere presence had brightened up his day, and I'm sure, that of the entire ward, too. When we had been visiting Bill, we'd noticed her. She always had a smile and a cheery word for each patient. The ward was very short-staffed that day, but she still took time to stop and ask whether they needed anything.

There is marvellous modern equipment in hospitals nowadays, and we thank God for it, but we still need the personal touch and tender loving care of nurses like Joanna.

SATURDAY—NOVEMBER 20.

SUE RYDER, who, with her husband Group Captain Leonard Cheshire, established Homes in 44 different countries to relieve the suffering of disabled and incurably sick people, once wrote:

"Think deeply, speak gently, love much, laugh often, work hard, give freely, pay promptly, pray earnestly and be kind."

What a wealth of wisdom she packed into one short sentence!

SUNDAY—NOVEMBER 21.

THE Lord is good, a strong hold in the day of trouble; and he knoweth them that trust in him.
Nahum 1:7

THE FRIENDSHIP BOOK

IT could happen to any of us.

There was the bridegroom, standing at the altar of a village church and understandably nervous. Three times he managed to say "I will" — twice in the wrong place.

When the marriage ceremony was over, and the bridal pair had retired to the vestry to sign the register, the vicar expressed the hope that he would have a very happy married life.

"Same to you, sir," stammered the bridegroom, "and many of 'em!"

THIS poem, dedicated by Dorothy Una Ratcliffe to her godson, gives thanks for all God's gifts:

God, Darling! Listen to my song,
The one I sing the whole day long,
Of thanks to Thee for every good,
Whether at home, in field, or wood.

I thank Thee for the lovely Spring,
And for Thy little birds that sing;
I thank Thee for the Summer's sun,
When 'mong the roses I can run.

I thank Thee for the sickle time,
When corn is ripe, and apples prime;
I thank Thee for the deep white snow,
When I tobogganing can go.

I thank Thee for the bright sweet day,
For hours of love and work and play;
I thank Thee for the deep blue night
When I and flower-buds fold up tight.

THE FRIENDSHIP BOOK

A YORKSHIREMAN wanted an inscription on his wife's gravestone. He felt that "She Was Thine" would be sufficient, and instructed the mason accordingly. However the engraver made a mistake, and the finished result read: "She was Thin".

The Yorkshireman wrote to the mason pointing out that he had missed out the "E". The mason got to work again. The amended result read: "E, She was Thin"!

TODAY is St Catherine's Day. Did you know that she is the patron saint of spinners, weavers and lacemakers?

Pillow, or bobbin lace, was said to be invented in Saxony in the 16th century. By the following century it had spread through Europe. Places such as Brussels, Valenciennes, Honiton and Nottingham became famous for their beautiful lace.

There is a lovely old story told in Bruges that a woman lay seriously ill and her daughter prayed for a miracle to provide food, warmth and comfort. Suddenly, her eye caught a perfectly-formed spider's web in the corner of the room.

She was a skilled needlewoman so she picked up her thread and tried to copy the web, but her thread kept getting tangled. Then she realised that if she secured each strand to a separate little stick, she could weave the threads to resemble the spider's web without any tangling.

This way she was able to get on quickly with her work, and they say that her discovery was the beginning of the bobbin lacemaking for which the city of Bruges is famous.

PERFECT MORNING

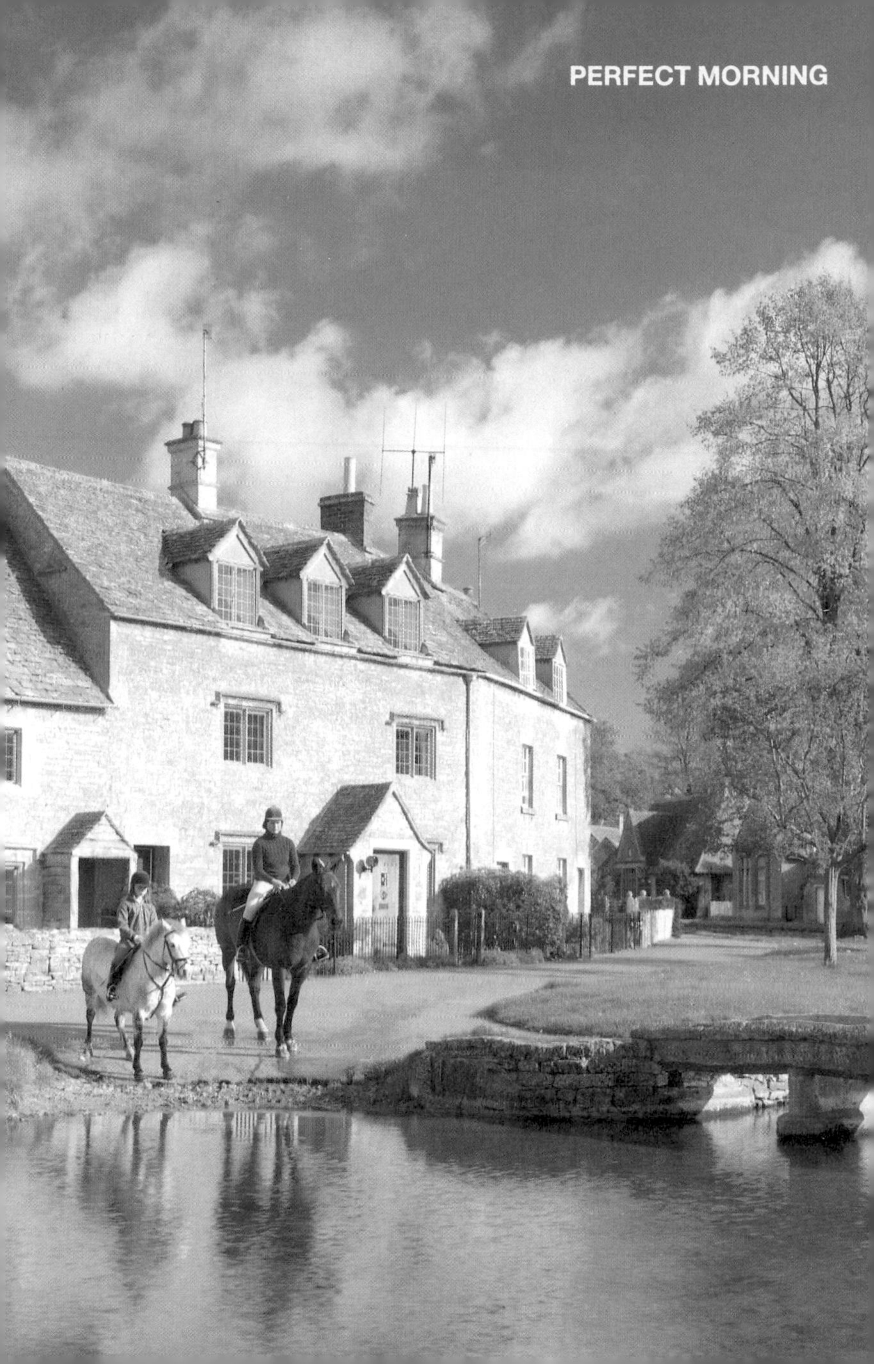

FRIDAY—NOVEMBER 26.

THIS little verse has been passed on to me by a friend and has given me quite a lot to think about:

> *The future lies before you*
> *Like a field of driven snow,*
> *Be careful how you tread it,*
> *For every step will show.*

It's something you, too, might like to ponder at the start of another day, and I would commend it to anyone starting a new job, moving to a new neighbourhood or facing any sort of fresh situation. Tread carefully, but with confidence, and the footprints you leave will be clear and firm.

SATURDAY—NOVEMBER 27.

TOMORROW is Advent Sunday — the day when Christians think of the coming of Christ; the day when the Christian Calendar begins again, and when we think of the Light that shone in our darkness.

I wonder if you know the story of the father who willed that his fortune should be left to the one of his three sons who should most successfully fill a room with anything that cost no more than a shilling.

One son tried to fill it with bricks, but managed to fill only a very small part. The second son bought straw, the cheapest thing he could think of, and managed to half-fill the room. The third son bought a small candle, and filled the room with light.

SUNDAY—NOVEMBER 28.

ARISE, shine; for thy light is come, and the glory of the Lord is risen upon thee.

Isaiah 60:1

THE FRIENDSHIP BOOK

TWO newcomers to our neighbourhood went to a coffee morning in aid of a local charity. The first lady came away feeling very disgruntled. "What an unfriendly lot they are," she complained. "I sat on my own all morning and nobody came to speak to me. I won't bother going again."

The other lady went home happily. "I wanted to get to know people," she said, "and I soon got chatting to some of the helpers. They're such nice people. I'm going to join them and I've offered to bake some cakes the next time they have a coffee morning."

So often, what we look for is what we get!

"I'VE passed it dozens of times tucked away in the vestry and never really noticed it until recently. I took it for granted," commented a friendly voluntary guide at Holy Trinity, Skipton's ancient church.

She was referring to an ancient wooden arched door surround which had been cleaned and erected as an entrance to the new flower room off the chancel.

On the arch were inscribed the names of people — some going back to the 15th century — who had left possessions to bring comfort to less fortunate people. The names, dates and facts made compelling reading. More interesting still were the guide's words, "took it for granted".

Isn't it something we do in so many spheres of life? We are all given to taking so many things for granted. Our health; the pleasure brought by beautiful flowers and wildlife; the kindness of our friends and neighbours . . . The list is endless.

Just recalling all the small happinesses we take for granted makes life so much richer for other people and for ourselves, too.

DECEMBER

COLD, Winter days are perhaps the least liked in the calendar. However, as this verse shows, the outlook at this time of year is far from bleak:

The wind blows chill, the year grows old,
* December's here once more,*
And sure the days will colder grow
* And wilder winds will roar.*
But, God be thanked, December brings
* Again the Christmas spell —*
When hearts are warmed and hopes are bright
* And faith says "All is well."*

WHEN Dr John G. Paton became a missionary to the islands of the New Hebrides in the Pacific, he set to work translating the Bible into the local tongue. To his surprise he couldn't find a suitable word meaning to "trust".

He went to see one of the older women, sat in a chair with his feet on the floor, and asked her what he was doing. "Resting," she replied, but that was not the word he was looking for.

Dr Paton raised his feet from the floor and put them on the cross-piece between the chair's front legs. "Now what am I doing?" he asked.

In reply the woman used a native word which meant to recline one's whole weight upon something — a word he had never heard before.

That was it! — the word he wanted, to describe trusting in Jesus — and he was now able to complete his translation.

THE FRIENDSHIP BOOK

MARJORY is over 80. She used to work in a needlework shop, and has a gift for embroidery. She designed kneelers for her church and still helps local people with their crafts. In fact, all her leisure time is spent giving unpaid service to others.

Last Summer she was asked if she would design a central motif for her village Christmas decorations. It was no easy task and Marjory worried about it, until one morning she spilled some porridge on to her tiled kitchen floor. There in the splodge she could see the elusive design she wanted — a spiral star!

The villagers clapped and cheered as the Christmas lights were switched on. Marjory was watching, too, seeing the happy children's faces, the bright stars in the frosty sky, and thanking God for the accident that had been the inspiration for this wonderful moment. That simple household incident had been transformed into beauty.

BETSY BROWN was, I remember, one of the "characters" in our street when I was young. Never over-blessed with the world's goods, she nevertheless spread around her own brand of riches.

"I always thank the Lord," she would say, "for the things I HAVEN'T got! A smoking chimney, a leaky roof, rheumaticky joints and troublesome neighbours!"

FOR he is not a God of the dead, but of the living: for all live unto him.

Luke 20:38

THE FRIENDSHIP BOOK

SEEING in a magazine the illustration of a Christmas table laden with food and wine, it set me thinking about the place that tables occupy in our lives.

What marvellous work is carried out every day on an operating table under the skilful hands of a surgeon! We all have reason to be grateful for that table.

One of my favourites is the kitchen table, with its well-scrubbed top. How I loved to sit beside it as a child and talk over with my mother my day at school!

Then there is the Round Table, housed in the Great Hall at Winchester. Here it is said, King Arthur and his knights met to eat and plan valiant deeds. The present day "Round Tablers" are made up of young men from all professions, who also meet to dine and plan schemes to help their local community.

I have left the most special table until last — the Communion table, which means so much to Christians. It, surely, is the greatest table of all.

HARRY KEATING of Toronto, Ontario, sent me these three thoughts from his scrapbook:

A man must prove many things to many people; foremost, he must prove himself to himself.

Blessed is he who has mastered the art of writing, or painting, sculpture or the stage. Even more blessed is he who has mastered the art of love.

How is it that "I" is always capitalised, while "you" is not? Are You not as important as I?

THE FRIENDSHIP BOOK

CHRISTMAS is coming . . . how do you prepare
for it? These lines from G. L. Mokrzycka of
Perth may help:

Now cast aside your feeling of frustration,
  Ignore the daily ups and downs of life,
For this is now a time of jubilation,
  As Christmas bells ring out to quell the strife.
Begin inside your heart with love for others,
  Share your family circle's joy with friends,
Reach outward to embrace the broken-hearted,
  And where words have wounded — make amends.

THERE are two small words in our English
language which we use every day. In some
respects they are alike in meaning, and yet are
profoundly different — they are "go" and "come".

"Oh, yes," a person might reply to an enquiry: "Go
down there." So we go — alone — perhaps into the
unknown. Suppose, though, the reply was, "Come,
I'll show you," we would then feel secure, for the word
"come" gives assurance. The person knows the way, is
familiar with it, and will accompany us.

What has this to do with the Christmas season?
Just this — it's a wonderful time to witness to our faith
and invite others to find the One who was born at
Bethlehem. To searching people, we can say, "Jesus
Christ is the way. Come with me to Bethlehem." To
fearful people we can say, "Don't be afraid. Come with
me to Bethlehem." To confused people we can say,
"There is good news. Come with me to Bethlehem."

How much more reassuring, personal and
convincing it is to hear, "Come with me" rather than
"Go that way."

THE FRIENDSHIP BOOK

I HAVE just found this little story and I thought that you would like it, too.

A minister once visited an elderly gentleman who was stone-deaf and very ill. After a while, the minister suggested that he should say a prayer. The parishioner's wife said, "Eric will never hear you."

The minister kindly, and very simply replied, "It's not Eric I'll be talking to."

EARLY in December, letters start arriving from relatives and friends we perhaps haven't seen for many years, but with whom we make a point of keeping in touch at least once in the year. As we recognise the writing on the envelope, it is opened with great anticipation.

Some are brief messages written on the back of a Christmas card, whilst others, packed with news of the past year, have obviously been typed then duplicated and sent out to a wide circle of people.

I must admit that the letters we most enjoy receiving are the ones specially written for us — those which describe something the writer knows will particularly interest us, or which send me a message of comfort or encouragement.

When we receive such letters, we are delighted, for we can picture the sender, realising that distance alone can never destroy true friendship.

SING praises to the Lord, which dwelleth in Zion: declare among the people his doings.

Psalms 9:11

N

THE FRIENDSHIP BOOK

DURING the American War of Independence, George Washington was friendly with a minister called Peter Miller. Miller had an enemy in the town where he lived, a man called Michael Wittman, who did everything he could to oppose him.

Wittman was eventually arrested for treason and sentenced to death.

When he heard what had happened, Miller walked 70 miles to Philadelphia to plead for his life. He begged Washington to give Wittman a pardon and set him free.

"No, Peter," said Washington, "I cannot grant you the life of your friend."

"My friend!" exclaimed Peter. "He's the worst enemy I have." Washington looked at him in amazement. "You have walked all these miles to save an enemy? That puts a different light on the matter — I will pardon him!"

From that day, Wittman was no longer Miller's enemy, but a true friend.

CAESAR AUGUSTUS was Emperor of Rome at the time of the birth of Christ. It came to his knowledge that a certain Roman had accumulated a heavy debt without anyone knowing about it.

After the man's death, Augustus ordered that his pillow should be purchased for his own use. When eyebrows were raised and surprise expressed, he explained, "The pillow on which he could sleep with all those debts must be specially comfortable."

It's an interesting story, though the fact remains that probably the best formula for sleep is a clear conscience and an untroubled mind.

THE FRIENDSHIP BOOK

KAY THOMSON, a reader in South Africa, sent me this thoughtful little poem, to share with you as we prepare to celebrate the festive season:

> *Count your garden by the flowers,*
> *Never by the leaves that fall.*
> *Count your joys by golden dreams,*
> *Never when life's worries call.*
> *Count your nights by stars, not shadows,*
> *Count your days by smiles, not tears.*
> *And, on every Christmas morning,*
> *Count your age by friends, not years.*

ONE Winter, the city of Florence was severely flooded. The inhabitants were anxious about the effects of water damage on their ancient cathedral, but they had to wait until Midsummer's Day for the verdict. This day was chosen for a special reason by its first architect, to test its stability. On Midsummer Day a solitary sunbeam filters through a hole in the dome, and should gleam for a moment on a brass plate. If it does, all is well, but if it does not, the foundations have moved. You can tell by the beam of light.

Life, too, can be like this. Darkness can descend upon us, maybe for a considerable time. Everything seems to go wrong. It may be through the death of a loved one, illness or unemployment.

Then suddenly, a sunbeam shines through, it gradually strengthens us and we find that life becomes brighter again. We know that the light comes from a special source and that our "foundations" are safe, no matter what may happen.

FRIDAY—DECEMBER 17.

I REMEMBER the days when nearly every young schoolboy wanted to be an engine driver when he grew up. For some of us, the desire lingers on and we can still be thrilled by the sight of an old-time locomotive in full steam.

This thought struck me as I was reading some words about middle age recently. Kim Hubbard wrote: "Boys will be boys — and so will a lot of middle-aged men!" William Feather said, "Setting a good example for your children takes all the fun out of middle age."

SATURDAY—DECEMBER 18.

ON my desk is a photograph of a smiling face. It warms my heart, gives me strength, and helps me to get my priorities right.

It is a colour snapshot of a Tibetan gentleman spinning wool in a very primitive way. His clothes are tattered, and he is obviously very poor, but in spite of the hard life he must lead, he is smiling happily — a genuine, lovely, contented smile. His lined face and hands tell of his life of toil, but that smile means such a lot. Most of all, it tells me that despite hardships he is a very contented man.

Each morning I look at him and try to absorb some of his contentment. I cannot have his hands, or his eyes, or the same smile, but I *can* have a contented heart like his, if I try — and so can you.

SUNDAY—DECEMBER 19.

HEAL me, O Lord, and I shall be healed; save me, and I shall be saved: for thou art my praise.

Jeremiah 17:14

CALL OF THE HILLS

THE FRIENDSHIP BOOK

HERE is another "Thought for the Week" from the church newsletter which a friend sends me from time to time:

> I am only one, but I *am* one;
> I cannot do everything
> But I can do something.
> What I can do, I ought to do,
> And what I ought to do,
> By the grace of God I *will* do.

THIS charming Christmas poem was sent to me by Jean Harris, of Stockton-on-Forest:

> *"See His hands," said the donkey,*
> *"So fragile and small,*
> *Yet offering the Truth of the World*
> *To us all."*
>
> *"See His feet," said the grey sheep,*
> *"His tiny toes curled,*
> *Yet one day they will lead*
> *The Way for the World."*
>
> *"See His eyes," said the brown ox,*
> *"His sweet, gentle face,*
> *The Light of the World*
> *Is here by God's grace."*
>
> *"See His Love," said the donkey,*
> *"It shines like a light,*
> *Round His head like a halo,*
> *Let's praise God tonight."*

THE FRIENDSHIP BOOK

WE often smile — or find deeply moving — some of the things children write to Santa Claus. Here is something I came across recently, written, I suspect, by a rather more grown-up child!:

Where is Santa Claus?
He's seen in the smiles the whole world is sharing;
He's found where there's friendship and loving and
caring;
He's felt in warm handshakes when people are
meeting;
He's heard in the cheer of a Christmas-time
greeting;
And his spirit's behind all the gifts we receive,
He's everywhere, always, to those who believe.

AT the John Coram Foundling Hospital in London, there is a portrait of Coram, painted by the famous artist William Hogarth.

John and William were good friends, and both in their own way tried to help the poor children of the time on London's streets. William was one of the first people to foster a child from the hospital, while John and others cared for and helped many others.

Hogarth was once asked which of his prolific paintings he liked best. "The one of John Coram," he replied. In those days it was usual to be dressed for the occasion when being painted. Men would wear — often hired — periwigs and bright silk waistcoats, but not John Coram. Hogarth portrayed his friend in his working clothes with no adornments.

As a painter, Hogarth knew that character is to be found in the face and in the heart, not by wearing fashionable clothes. He admired the truth.

FRIDAY—DECEMBER 24.

HERE is a very true saying that I noted some time ago:

"Feed your faith and your doubts will starve to death."

SATURDAY—DECEMBER 25.

THERE are many legends about the birth of Jesus, but I particularly like this one about Jacob the shepherd boy.

He was the youngest of the shepherds and when the angel appeared to proclaim the birth of Christ, he went with the other shepherds to see the new-born King. At the manger they knelt and worshipped him, and then went away to tell the good news to their friends. Only Jacob stayed behind, still lost in wonder.

As the night grew colder, Mary took off her cloak and wrapped it around her baby, while Jacob held his lamp high to warm the air above the crib. All night he stood there, holding his lamp, and when dawn came he smiled at the Mother and the Christ Child before leaving the stable.

Then a strange thing happened. He tried to blow out the lamp, but he couldn't. It went on burning brightly and it continued to burn until the very end of his life, as a token, they say, of his loving act on that first Christmas night.

SUNDAY—DECEMBER 26.

BEHOLD, a virgin shall be with child, and shall bring forth a son, and they shall call his name Emmanuel, which being interpreted is, God with us.

Matthew 1:23

WHAT DO YOU THINK?

THE FRIENDSHIP BOOK

I'M sure you must have noticed the large wrought-iron gates, often chained, that guard the entrances to large houses or stately homes. I watched with interest as a postman approached such a house, and I wondered how he would get inside the huge, imposing gates. He simply opened and stepped through a small gate set into one of the large ones. It was so easy.

It isn't necessary for us to make a grand entrance through the large gate, to make our mark in the world. For every person who is outwardly and loudly successful, there are many more folk equally successful in a quiet, unassuming way. Their work behind the scenes is very necessary for the smooth running of our world.

Most of us are "small gate" people and happy to be so, doing our work, whatever it is, without a great deal of recognition, to the best of our ability. The satisfaction of knowing that we have done our best, is reward enough.

MY thanks to Barbara Jemison, Bridlington, for these lines, packed with wisdom:

The more you give, the more you get,
The more you laugh, the less you fret;
The more you do unselfishly,
The more you live abundantly;
The more of everything you share,
The more you'll always have to spare;
The more you love, the more you'll find
That life is good and friends are kind;
For only what we give away,
Enriches us from day to day.

THE FRIENDSHIP BOOK

"HELLO, Mr Gay," said my young neighbour Billy when I met him on the way home from school. "Can you tell me how many weeks a year has?"

"Yes, Billy, that's an easy one," I replied at once. "A year has 52 weeks."

"Wrong, Mr Gay," chuckled Billy. "It has only 46. The other six are 'Lent'!"

THE writer George MacDonald once remarked: "If instead of a gem or even a flower, we could cast the gift of a lovely thought into the heart of a friend, that would be giving as the angels give."

It's a good phrase for us all to reflect upon today.

"IT'S no wonder I couldn't pick up all the bits from the carpet, Francis," remarked the Lady of the House recently. "When I looked inside the vacuum cleaner, I could see that its dustbag was so packed that it couldn't possibly hold any more, but what a difference I noticed next morning once it had a new bag inside! I seemed to clean round the house in no time at all."

It's just like life, isn't it? We allow ourselves to get cluttered up with so many things — half-finished tasks, good intentions that never materialise, relationships with others that could be improved upon. Isn't it good to know that each day we can have a fresh beginning — particularly when we stand on the threshold of another year.

As Benjamin Franklin said, "Be at war with your vices, at peace with your neighbours, and let every New Year find you a better man or woman."

Where The Photographs Were Taken

TIMELESS — *River Medway, Aylesford, Kent.*

HEAVENLY HEIGHTS — *Norwich Cathedral.*

FINISHING TOUCH — *Brayford Pool, Lincoln.*

ADVENTURE BOUND — *Tarn Hows, Lancashire.*

A PLACE TO PONDER — *Derwent Water, Cumbria.*

APRIL MORN — *Borrowdale, Cumbria.*

LAZY AFTERNOON — *The Backs, Cambridge.*

CLIMBER'S REWARD — *On Cruach Ardrain, Perthshire.*

HIGH DAYS ON HOLIDAY — *Weymouth Beach, Dorset.*

FAMILY GATHERINGS — *Pulls Ferry, Norwich.*

EXPLORERS — *The River Cam, near Cambridge.*

MARIGOLD COTTAGE — *Shamley Green, Surrey.*

SEA, SAND AND SUN — *Bournemouth.*

BLUE HORIZON — *Land's End.*

COUNTRY DELIGHT — *Lorna Doone Farm, Devon.*

CAREFREE — *Above Swaledale, Yorkshire.*

HISTORIC WATERS — *Bath.*

PERFECT MORNING — *Lower Slaughter, Gloucestershire.*

HIGH ENDEAVOUR — *Ratcliffe Square, Oxford.*

CALL OF THE HILLS — *Loch Lomond From Conic Hill.*

ACKNOWLEDGEMENTS: **David Askham;** Alert, What Do You Think? **Ivan Belcher;** Timeless, Steam Symphony, A Place To Ponder, Golden Girl, Lazy Afternoon, Ahoy There!, High Days On Holiday, Family Gatherings, Sea Sand And Sun, Blue Horizon, Country Delight, Historic Waters. **V.B. Hicks;** Climber's Reward. **Dennis Mansell;** Looking To The Future, Explorers, Carefree, Call Of The Hills. **Picturepoint Ltd.;** Adventure Bound. **Clifford Robinson;** Heavenly Heights. **Kenneth Scowen;** Gift Of Gold, Secret Glade, Cool Harvest. **Andy Williams;** Finishing Touch, April Morn, Marigold Cottage, Ready!, Perfect Morning, High Endeavour.

Printed and Published by D. C. THOMSON & CO., LTD.,
185 Fleet Street, London EC4A 2HS.
© D. C. THOMSON & Co., Ltd., 1992

ISBN 0-85116-551-6